# Bruges
## & Ghent

# TOP 10 ATTRACTIONS

**The Begijnhof** • A peaceful retreat in the heart of the city *(page 39)*

**Canals** • Cruising the waterways is a relaxing way to enjoy the historic sights *(page 11)*

**Onze-Lieve-Vrouwekerk** • One of Bruges's finest churches *(page 36)*

**Memling in Sint-Jan** • Houses the excellent Memling Museum *(page 38*

**Gravensteen** · A 12th-century fortress in the heart of Ghent (page 78)

**is Ter Beurze** · An gant 15th-century nsion (page 53)

**Stadhuis** · The gilded Gothic Town Hall (page 28)

**oeninge Museum** · Works by Flemish masters (page 34)

**ll Tower** · The 13th-ntury structure looms er the city (page 27)

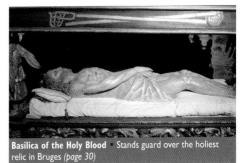

**Basilica of the Holy Blood** · Stands guard over the holiest relic in Bruges (page 30)

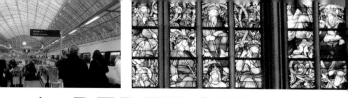

# A PERFECT DAY

**9.00am** **Breakfast**

Go to the Art Nouveau De Medici Sorbetière at Geldmuntstraat 9 for breakfast in a splendid setting.

**12.30pm** **Lunch**

A good traditional restaurant is Breydel-De Coninck (tel: 050-33 97 46), in Breidelstraat. For something more sophisticated, go down Blinde-Ezelstraat and cross the canal to the Vismarkt (Fish Market), to the highly regarded seafood restaurant De Visscherie (tel: 050-33 02 12).

**11.00am** **The Burg**

The historic square contains the Romanesque Heilig-Bloedbasiliek, the lovely Gothic Stadhuis and the Baroque Proosdij.

**2.00pm** **Groeninge**

Go along the canal on photogenic Rozenhoedkaai and tree-shaded Dijver, then turn left into Groeninge. If you visit only one museum in Bruges, this should be it, for its world-class collection of paintings by the medieval Flemish Primitives – Jan van Eyck, Hans Memling, Rogier van der Weyden, Gerard David and others.

**10.00am** **The Markt**

Stroll into the nearby Markt, for a turn around the magnificent market square. You will take in Belfort and Hallen, and medieval buildings that have hosted kings and emperors, plus a bustle of cafés, restaurants and bars.

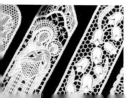

# N BRUGES

### 4.30pm Towards the Begijnhof

Next to the museum, the Gothic Onze-Lieve-Vrouwekerk is worth visiting for its *Madonna and Child* sculpture by Michelangelo. Across the street is Memling in Sint-Jan, a collection of works by Hans Memling. By way of the Halve Maan Brewery, you arrive at the pretty courtyard of the Begijnhof, now a Benedictine convent.

### 3.00pm Culture fix

If you fancy one more museum, or you missed out on the Groeninge, cross the canal on pretty little Boniface Bridge to the 15th-century Paleis van Gruuthuse, which hosts the Bruggemuseum-Gruuthuse, a fascinating historical museum.

### 8.00pm Dinner

If you want to dine in this area, off the north end of the Minnewater you will find the traditional Flemish restaurant Maximiliaan van Oostenrijk (tel: 050-33 47 23). Alternatively, return to the Vismarkt area, for dinner at Huidevettershuis (tel: 050-33 95 06), in a medieval guild house.

### 6.00pm The Lake of Love

Just south of the Begijnhof, the Minnewater lake probably takes its name from Bruges's medieval *Binnen Water* (Inner Harbour), but can be imaginatively translated as the 'Lake of Love'. On its east bank is a handsome park and the Kasteel Minnewater château. It is worth strolling around here and into neighbouring streets off the lake's eastern shore.

# CONTENTS

Features

95

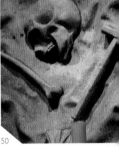

50

53

# INTRODUCTION

The land that is now Belgium has been coveted and fought over for thousands of years. The modern visitor can still catch the faint echo of all the armies that have battled and died on the soil of Flanders. Today, the nation that once was crisscrossed by foreign forces is traversed by millions of visitors – most of them on their way to holidays elsewhere in Europe. More and more travellers, however, are learning the secrets of Belgium, having discovered for themselves one of the country's greatest treasures – Bruges.

Those gabled houses, meandering canals, and narrow cobblestone streets combine to create one of Europe's most romantic towns. Misleading talk of the 'Venice of the North' or 'Belgium's Amsterdam' adds nothing to visitors' understanding or appreciation of Bruges. The pride of Flanders is unique – not some pale imitation of another place.

The history of the city is everywhere written in its streets and buildings, in its art and culture. Bruges, in particular, is justifiably famous for its sheer beauty. Indeed, there is an almost unreal quality to just how picturesque Bruges can be, as if in the Middle Ages the city had been a place of universal grace and effortless charm. Then there is the compact geography, which means that visitors can explore the city with ease on foot, by bike, and even on the water.

Water forms an important part of the landscape and economy of Bruges. Canals link the city to the coast and important industrial centres

## Getting around

There is no need for a car in Bruges: the city is compact and canalside roads and paths make for excellent walking and cycling.

Canalside buildings along the Langerei in Bruges

in Belgium and around Europe. A leisurely cruise along the canals is an experience not to be missed, and one of the best ways of viewing the wonderful cityscape.

It is, of course, people that constitute a city: there are about 120,000 in Bruges. Most of the population is Roman Catholic, and the virtues of community cohesion in work and play make up much of what it is to be Flemish. Tradition and family life are important, and people take their work and their pleasures seriously – which explains why Belgium produces more than 450 different beers.

Something else that figures prominently in Belgium are museums. The Belgians, at least in their civic life, have a passion for collecting and recording; Bruges shares this national characteristic, with some superb museums and galleries. It also has a rich calendar of events *(see page 94)*, including the spectacular Procession of the Holy Blood.

Eating and drinking are mostly hearty events and form an important part of life. Belgian cuisine is justly famous throughout the world, both for its quality and its quantity (you will never go hungry in Belgium), and there are plenty of fine restaurants in Bruges. An intrinsic part of everyday eating is the Belgian french fry *(friet)*, which is available everywhere, and often eaten with mayonnaise. Equally ubiq-

## Not Far Away

Belgium is a compact country (less than 325 km/200 miles across at its widest point), so nowhere is very far from anywhere else. Most of the other places of interest listed in this guide are within a few miles of Bruges or Ghent, themselves connected by a reliable half-hour train journey. Those places farther away are easily accessible, thanks to the country's superb railways – in 1835 Belgium ran the first train in continental Europe, and standards are still high.

Canal tours are a relaxed form of sightseeing

uitous are the exquisite Belgian chocolates you will see in mouth-watering shop displays.

The Belgians have a strong sense of pride in their achievements and their history. Bruges had a distinctive role in the development of the area. Before the foundation of the Belgian state in 1830, it was virtually an autonomous city-state. Nationhood itself is a fiercely debated issue in Belgium. Bruges is in Flanders, where the official language is Dutch, but a large proportion of the country is inhabited by French-speaking Walloons. In fact, the residents of Bruges nearly all speak English and French, as well as Dutch.

Bruges takes its visitors seriously. The tourist office is friendly and informative, and in cafés, bars and hotels you will be served courteously, with patience and good humour. Whether you are staying for a weekend or using the city as a base for a longer tour, Bruges will reward you with beauty, fascinating history and a warm welcome.

# A BRIEF HISTORY

The nation of Belgium only came into being in 1830, but Bruges can lay claim to a very long and distinguished history. The story of the region begins with the Belgae, a Celtic tribe who lived there from Neolithic times. In the first of many occupations throughout the centuries, the Belgae were conquered in 54BC by the Romans under Julius Caesar. His account of the conquest of Gaul, as it was known, is recorded in his *Gallic Wars*.

## The Kingdom of the Franks

With the decay of their empire early in the 5th century, the Romans withdrew from Gaul, much of which succumbed to the Franks, who had been settling in the region for the previous two centuries. They founded their Merovingian kingdom around Tournai in the south, while to the north and east the region was divided between Franks, Frisians and Saxons. The conversion to Christianity of the Frankish King Clovis in 498 led to a gradual northward spread of the new faith, until the whole region became Christian.

In 768, the Frankish king Charlemagne established a unified kingdom. By military and diplomatic means he went on to found a European empire, culminating in his coronation by the Pope in 800 as Emperor of the West. On his death in 814, the empire passed to his son Louis, and on Louis' death in 840 was divided between his three sons. The division left a narrow strip of Europe, including the Low Countries (Belgium, Luxem-

**Early record**

The first recorded mention of Bruges dates from the 8th century AD, though little is known about the town's origins, except that the name possibly comes from the Vikings.

bourg and the Netherlands), sandwiched between French- and German-speaking nations.

## The Golden Age of Bruges

The area came under the nominal rule of a succession of German and French kings, but real power was in the hands of local nobles, who tried to weaken the hold over them by the French and German feudal kingdoms. Some of these lords were more wealthy than their rulers and negotiated charters of autonomous rights for towns in exchange for taxes and military assistance.

Bruges begins to emerge from the Dark Ages around the mid-7th century, when St Eligius preached in coastal Flanders. Chronicles of his life refer to a Frankish community called the Municipium Flandrense, which seems to have been Bruges. Originally it was probably a Gallo-Roman port protected against Germanic sea-raiders by a *castellum* (fort) as the Roman Empire went into decline and fall. The first certain mention of Bruges occurs in 851 in records of monks from Ghent and by 864 the word 'Bruggia' appears on coins of Charles the Bald, king of the West Franks, to whom Flanders owed allegiance. Baldwin I

Rogier van der Weyden's portrait of Philip the Good

(known menacingly as Iron Arm), whose residence was a castle in the Burg in Bruges, is the first count of Flanders we know by name. He seems to have been a swashbuckler, eloping with Charles's daughter Judith and living to tell the tale.

Baldwin built a castle at Bruges in the 9th century, and from there pursued a fierce expansionist policy to establish the county of Flanders. In the 11th century, the succession passed to Robert the Frisian, who made Bruges his capital. Despite the ongoing power struggles, the cloth towns of Flanders flourished in the 12th and 13th centuries. Ghent became the largest town in Western Europe, while Bruges had a population as large as that of medieval London, trading with the Orient, the Middle East and the rest of Europe.

International banks made Bruges their headquarters, foreign embassies located there, and the first stock exchange in Europe was founded in the city. Wool was vital to the Flemish economy: Bruges, Ghent and Ypres (Ieper) all prospered from the export of their manufactured cloth, and depended for raw material on imported wool from England. Bruges monopolised the trade in wool and, as a result, came to trade with the Hanseatic League, a powerful economic alliance of trading towns in northern Europe. The prosperity of the city reached a peak early in the 14th century.

## Wealthy citizens

During what became known as the 'Joyful Entry' into Bruges in 1301, Queen Joan of Navarre marvelled at the rich apparel of the citizens: 'I thought I was the only queen, but there are hundreds more around me!'

But tension grew between the merchants, who had every reason for keeping in with the king of English (because he controlled the supply of wool) and their lords, who usually sided with the French king. In the 13th and 14th centuries, the cloth towns of Flanders were the scene of frequent hostilities. The city walls, the outline of which is preserved in the ring canal and its park, were built during the 14th century. Four of the nine original gates survive today, powerful bastions that give some idea of the strength of these defences.

The most famous conflict became known as the 'Bruges Matins'. The French king, Philip the Fair, had invaded Flanders and appointed a governor whose taxation and suppression of the powerful guilds of Bruges were so severe that on the night of 17–18 May 1302 the city revolted, led by Pieter de Coninck and Jan Breydel. The resentful rebels killed everyone they

A 15th-century painting of a Bruges goldsmith in his shop

believed to be French. In the same year the French were also defeated by the Flemish, at the Battle of the Golden Spurs near Kortrijk (Courtrai).

In 1384 the region became part of the Burgundian realm. Duke Philip the Good of Burgundy became count of Flanders in 1419 and ushered in a new kind of rule. He administered his possessions in Burgundy from Bruges, and was the patron of numerous artists, including Jan van Eyck and Hans Memling; the court became renowned for its splendour. In 1429 Philip received his fiancée, Isabella of Portugal, in Bruges – the cause for a celebration of sumptuous ostentation.

Charles the Bold, Philip's successor, and his bride Margaret

Charles the Bold of Burgundy

of York enjoyed a lavish wedding in Bruges when, it was said, the fountains spouted Burgundian wine. However, the splendour of Charles's reign did not last, and his death precipitated another French invasion of the south of the Low Countries. The people of Flanders took the opportunity to kidnap Charles's daughter Mary, forcing her in a charter to renew their civic rights (curtailed by Philip) before they would help fight the French.

## The Habsburgs

Maximilian of Austria married Mary and assumed full control of the region immediately after her death in 1482. The era of the powerful Habsburgs had begun. The burghers of Bruges still had the nerve to incarcerate Maximilian himself briefly in 1488, exacting further promises to acknowledge their rights, but Maximilian reneged on these as soon as he was released. His grandson Charles V, born in Ghent in 1500, continued a policy of favouring Antwerp rather than the cloth towns of Flanders – despite Bruges' reception of him amid great pomp and splendour in 1520. Charles' policy accelerated the economic decline of Bruges, which now had to contend with stiff competition from the cloth manufacturers in England. Bruges' death knell came when the River Zwin silted up, cutting off the town from the sea and ending its international trade; it did not awake from its economic slumber until the 19th century.

## The Reformation

The movement we call the Reformation was bound to have strong appeal for the merchants and people of Flanders. It stressed the rights of individuals to read and interpret the Word of God for themselves, thanks to the invention of the printing press, and questioned the clergy's power to promulgate a world view controlled by an alliance of State and Church. With the emergence of Luther and Calvin, pressure for reform turned into outright revolt, leading to the establishment of alternative churches. Protestantism was born.

The Low Countries were particularly receptive to new ideas, as rich merchants chafed against the strictures of a rigidly hierarchical social system, while the artisanal guilds had always resented any royal authority.

Charles V's abdication in 1555 meant that the Low Countries passed to his Catholic son, Philip II of Spain, and bloody conflict ensued. Philip and his sister Margaret harshly repressed Protestantism and tried to reinstate the authority of the Catholic Church. The 1565 harvest failure caused widespread famine and led to the Iconoclastic Fury, when workers ran riot among the Catholic churches, sacking and destroying everything. Frightened for their own positions, the nobility sided with Margaret and Philip. In 1567 Philip sent an army to the Low Countries. The 'Pacification of

### Trade Centre

The city's early prosperity depended on its role as the chief port of Flanders, a hub of the English and Scandinavian trade. From the Roman period to the 11th century, ships sailed right into the centre of town on the River Reie. Later, seagoing ships went as far as Damme, from where smaller vessels handled canal traffic with Bruges. It was one of the most important textile centres in northwest Europe.

Ghent', signed in the city in 1576, instated a short-lived period of peace and freedom of worship.

A subsequent war between the Spanish and the Dutch Protestants, led by William the Silent, resulted in the Low Countries being partitioned in 1579, with the Protestant north ultimately gaining independence and the Catholic south siding with the Spanish. This partition corresponds more or less to today's border between Belgium and the Netherlands.

## War of the Spanish Succession

The Habsburg dynasty in Spain ended in 1700 when Charles II died without an heir. He had specified that Philip V of Anjou should succeed him, but the Habsburg Leopold II of Austria had other ideas. He did not like the thought of the grandson of the king of France ruling Spain, thus uniting the two kingdoms under one dynasty. He was prepared to fight for this belief and the resulting war lasted from 1701 to 1714.

The treaty that ended the war signed over the Spanish Netherlands (now Belgium) to Austrian rule. They remained in Austrian hands under Archduchess Maria Theresa, and prospered through an arrangement whereby trade was subsidised by Austria.

Bruges' history is told in murals in the Stadhuis (Town Hall)

In 1780, Maria Theresa was succeeded by her son Joseph II. He fancied himself as a radical ruler and did institute several enlightened, secularising reforms, but his lack of consultation and his 'top-down' approach to change created widespread resentment. Sporadic rebellions occurred from 1788, and in 1790 the 'United States of Belgium' was proclaimed, winning recognition from Britain and the Netherlands. The fledgling nation was defeated a year later by the forces of the new Austrian Emperor, Leopold II.

## French Invasion and Independence

Despite having received military assistance from a Belgian contingent against the Austrians in 1792, the army of revolutionary France invaded Belgium and the Netherlands two years later and occupied the annexed countries for the next 20 years – though not without some benefit to Belgium. The country was divided into a number of *départements* along French lines; important and unjust aspects of Church, State, and taxation were reformed or abolished. There was also rapid subsidised industrialisation, with France being the main market for Belgian manufactured goods.

## Literary Revival

In literature, the 19th century saw something of a flourish in Flanders. Hendrik Conscience's 1838 novel *De Leeuw van Vlaanderen (The Lion of Flanders)* re-examined the revolt against the French in 1302, when a Flemish peasant army slaughtered the flower of French chivalry at the Battle of the Golden Spurs. Georges Rodenbach's 1892 novel *Bruges-la-Morte (Dead Bruges)* resonates with the air of mystery and decay into which Bruges had declined. Charles de Coster's *The Glorious Adventures of Tijl Uilenspiegel* (1867) provided neighbouring Damme with its legendary local hero. The Catholic priest Guido Gezelle breathed new life into Flemish poetry with his volumes *Kerkhofblommen (Graveyard Flowers*, 1858), *Tijdkrans (Time's Garland*, 1893) and *Rijmsnoer (String of Rhymes*, 1897), poems dealing with nature, religion and Flemish nationalism, in a mixture of literary Dutch and West Flanders dialect.

Yet no country likes to be controlled by another. Rebellions broke out from 1798 onwards. Following the final defeat of Napoleon at the Battle of Waterloo in 1815, the Congress of Vienna perpetuated Belgium's subjugation by giving control to the Dutch House of Orange. It was not until the revolution in 1830 that an autonomous free Belgian state was created. In 1831, the London Conference recognised the independence of Belgium and established it as a constitutional monarchy. Leopold I was awarded the crown.

## Armageddon – Twice

Throughout the 19th century, Belgium modernised, immersing itself in the Industrial Revolution. Slowly, Bruges was being rediscovered by British travellers on their way to the site of the Battle of Waterloo. Ghent revived, becoming a major economic centre. Yet tensions between different linguistic groups became more obvious as social difficulties failed to be resolved. In need of a scapegoat, the predominantly Dutch-speaking (and increasingly prosperous) north agitated for independence from the (French-speaking) Walloon south. Instead of attending to the problems of his country, the new king of Belgium, Leopold II (1865–1909) devoted most of his time to personal interests, including a private colony in the Belgian Congo. In 1909 his nephew succeeded him, as Albert I.

### Famine in Flanders

In the mid-19th century, living conditions for working people were appalling, aggravated by a dreadful famine in Flanders from 1845 to 1848. Almost half the population of Bruges was dependent on charity.

During Albert's reign, World War I gripped Belgium for four years. In 1914, the German army invaded, despite the country's neutrality, forcing the king to move to a narrow remaining strip of unoccupied Belgium. His resistance to the invaders gained him international renown as the 'Soldier King'.

The war's northern front extended roughly diagonally across the country, with the most infamous, and bloodiest, of battles taking place around Ypres (Ieper) in western Flanders. The defeat of Germany won Belgium considerable reparations and some new territory.

It might have been expected that the experience of war would draw the nation together, especially when King Albert proclaimed a series of

The Menin Gate in Ypres pays tribute to the war dead

reforms meant to improve equality between the Flemish and the Walloons. But as fascism was already working its way through both communities, they grew more antagonistic. In 1940, the German army marched into Belgium, occupying it in just three weeks. Bruges suffered little damage, though its new canal had to be repaired extensively.

A resistance movement formed, including an underground network to protect Belgium's Jews. However, the behaviour of the king, Leopold III, who was eager to accommodate the invaders, caused much controversy after the war as Belgium sought to rebuild itself. In 1950, the people voted by a narrow margin to ask the king home from exile, but Leopold decided to abdicate in favour of his son, Baudouin I.

## Regionalisation

After forming Benelux, an economic union with the Netherlands and Luxembourg, Belgium went on to join the European

Economic Community in 1957, with Brussels the seat of the organisation. Though this has ensured that Belgium is internationally recognised as the home of European bureaucracy, it has nevertheless retained its own distinct national character.

The country finally divested itself of the Congo (now the Democratic Republic of Congo) in 1960. Internal political events since the end of World War II have been dominated by continuing friction between the Flemish and Walloons. In 1977, three federal regions were established – Wallonia, Flanders and Brussels – in an attempt to ease the tensions between the groups by giving them greater self-determination. In 1989, regional governments were created, each with responsibility for all policy except matters concerning social security, defence and foreign affairs. A new constitution was adopted in 1994, establishing Belgium as a federal state.

The solemn Procession of the Holy Blood

In practice, visitors will see little sign of intercommunity tension. Bruges' ambitious restoration of its medieval centre continues to attract tourists from all over the world. But it refuses to be pigeon-holed as a dead, medieval town, and is looking to the future. Several landmark buildings have recently been constructed, including the concert theatre, and Japanese architect Toyo Ito's pavilion on the Burg.

# Historical Landmarks

**58–51BC** Roman conquest of Gaul, including present-day Belgium.

**AD498** Conversion to Christianity of Frankish King Clovis.

**700s** First probable mention of Bruges.

**768** Charlemagne's unified Frankish kingdom is established.

**Early 800s** Castle (Burg) built at Bruges.

**814** Death of Charlemagne and division of empire.

**851** First certain mention of Bruges.

**864** Baldwin becomes first known Count of Flanders.

**11th century** Silting cuts off Bruges's access to the sea.

**1134** Storm creates Zwin inlet, restoring Bruges's access to the sea.

**1150** Count Thierry returns from Crusades with Relic of the Holy Blood.

**1302** Bruges Matins and Battle of the Golden Spurs.

**1384** Flanders becomes part of Burgundian kingdom.

**1419** Philip the Good of Burgundy becomes count of Flanders.

**1482** Habsburg reign begins with Maximilian of Austria.

**1520** Silting closes Zwin inlet, cutting off access to the sea again.

**1555** Charles V abdicates; Philip II of Spain succeeds.

**1567–79** Religious wars in the southern Low Countries.

**1780** Maria Theresa dies; Joseph II accedes.

**1790** Proclamation of United States of Belgium.

**1794** French invade and occupy country for 20 years.

**1815** Napoleon defeated at Waterloo; Congress of Vienna.

**1830** Belgian revolution and independence.

**1914–18** World War I; Germans invade neutral Belgium.

**1940** Nazi Germany occupies Belgium during World War II.

**1977** Establishment of Flanders as one of three federal Belgian regions.

**1993** Albert II becomes king of the Belgians.

**2002** The Concertgebouw concert and opera hall opens in the city.

**2005** De Halve Maan, the city's only brewery, launches a new beer, Brugse Zot.

**2008** Bruges is the setting for the hit black-comedy movie *In Bruges*.

**2012** Five-yearly historical festival, *Praalstoet van de Gouden Boom*.

# WHERE TO GO

Bruges is made for walking: it is very compact, with attractions clearly signposted. It has been dubbed the 'Venice of the North', and while this comparison is unfair to both places, it should come as no surprise that canal cruises are one of the best ways of viewing the city: central Bruges has 10km (6 miles) of canals, and 4km (2½ miles) of them are accessible by boat tour.

Bruges is the capital of West Flanders province, and Belgium's most popular tourist destination, so be prepared for large crowds in the summer. In describing the city's attractions, certain words spring to mind – 'charming', 'picturesque' and 'delightful', for instance. Bruges is all of these, which is why ambling through the city is such a pleasure. It is not built on a grand scale calculated to awe the visitor, but views crowd you on every side, and around each corner it seems there is something else to delight the eye and fire the imagination.

Paradoxically, it was Bruges' five centuries of economic decline that preserved the buildings we now enjoy – there was never any money to demolish and rebuild. The badly dilapidated city was 'discovered' by visitors in the 19th century, and in the quieter residential quarters you can still sense what it must have been like to walk through the forgotten streets of a forgotten town – your footsteps ringing on the cobblestones

Bruges' imposing Bell Tower

## Town centre

Bruges' Old Town is almost an island encircled by canals. At the centre of the island and at the heart of city life is the Markt, Bruges' main square. All the city sights described in this chapter are within 2 km (1 mile) of the Markt.

The neo-Gothic spires of the 19th-century Provinciaal Hof

while church bells chime and a horse's hooves echo from a nearby street.

One of the first things to strike visitors today is the harmonious appearance of the architecture. The characteristic step gables of the houses may be a bit worn through age, but this only adds to their charm. You will notice that most buildings are of brick, with their shutters and woodwork painted in traditional Bruges red. Bruges is now so beautifully restored that you may briefly find yourself yearning for something less perfect just by way of contrast; Belgians themselves describe the place as an outdoor museum.

Still, you are all but certain to enjoy the walk described below; you should also take pleasure in improvising by discovering the city on your own (perhaps simply following the canals, or tracing the path of the city walls with their big, imposing gates). Horse-drawn carriages can also be hired.

**❶** Our walk begins at the **Markt**, Bruges' main square. Before you set off, take time to look around the Markt. This may be the 21st century, but not much has changed since some of the civic buildings and houses that you can see were constructed; it's not hard to imagine what the place would have looked like in the city's bustling golden age, when merchants flocked here from all over Europe.

# SOUTH FROM THE MARKT

On the southeast side of the square, dominating the city, is the magnificent complex of brick buildings known as the **Belfort-Hallen** (Bell Tower and Covered Market; daily 9.30am–5pm; charge). One of the first priorities of any visitor is to ignore the 1m (3ft) lean of the 90m (300ft) belfry and climb its 366 steps for a breathtaking view of the town and surrounding countryside (the best time is early morning or late afternoon). The belfry dates from the 13th century, when Bruges was at the height of its prosperity, but the final storey (with the clock) is 15th-century. The second floor houses a treasury where the town seal and charters were kept safely behind intricate Romanesque grilles (built in 1292), each requiring nine separate keys to open them.

You may already have heard the 47-bell carillon (which weighs 27 tons and hangs in the tower above). The belfry is an excellent landmark when you're finding your way around. The covered market and courtyard, also dating from the 13th century, would have been crammed with traders, the air heavy with the scent of spices brought by Venetian merchants. A canal lay below the covered market, which was used for the loading and unloading of goods. City statutes were announced from the balcony over the market entrance.

The 13th-century cloth halls were once located on the east side of the Markt, now the site of the neo-Gothic **Provinciaal Hof**, housing the West Flanders provincial government (not open to visitors). The **Crae-nenburg**, on the opposite

## Bruges Matins

At the centre of the Markt is a 19th-century monument to the heroes of the Bruges Matins (see page 15). Pieter De Coninck and Jan Breydel are stained green with age, but they still look suitably determined.

side of the square, now an atmospheric café-brasserie, was where the Habsburg Crown Prince Maximilian of Austria was briefly imprisoned by the city in 1488. The future emperor, understandably disgruntled, did his best ever afterwards to promote trade through Antwerp at the expense of Bruges *(see page 16)*.

On the same side of the square, at the corner of Sint-Amandsstraat, is a beautiful 15th-century brick building, **Huis Bouchoute**. Restored in 1995 as closely as possible to its original brick Gothic – which entailed the removal of later rooftop crenellations – this house hosted the exiled English King Charles II in 1656–7. The roof-mounted octagonal compass and weathervane (1682) allowed Bruges merchants to judge their ships' chances of entering or leaving the port.

## The Burg

A stroll down Breidelstraat, in the southeast corner of the Markt (next to the Halle), takes you past narrow De Garre, the shortest street in Bruges; if you need refreshment, there's a cosy 100-beer bar at the end, the Staminee de Garre. Breidelstraat leads to the **Burg**, one of Europe's finest medieval squares, named after the castle built by Baldwin Iron Arm.

Which building in the square is the most splendid? It's a hard choice. On the corner of Breidelstraat and the Burg is the ornate Baroque **Proosdij** (Deanery), formerly the palace of the bishops of Bruges, dating from 1666. Its parapet is lined with urns and topped with a handsome female personification of justice armed with sword and scales. The building stands on the site of the demolished Sint-Donaaskerk (St Donatian's), a Carolingian-style church built around 950.

The **Stadhuis** (Town Hall; daily 9.30am–5pm; charge) on the south side of the Burg was constructed between 1376 and 1420. It is one of the oldest town halls in Belgium and a Gothic masterpiece, its delicately traced windows framed within pilasters topped with octagonal turrets. If you stand close to the building its statues and spiral chimneys seem to be curving down over you, and the detailing of the sandstone facade becomes even more impressive. The statues on the facade (modern copies of those painted by Van Eyck and destroyed by the French in the 1790s) are of the counts of Flanders.

The exterior of the Stadhuis promises great things, and the interior of the magnificent town hall will certainly not let you down. Bluestone stairs lead from the flag-draped entrance hall to the first-floor Gothic Hall,

The splendid Stadhuis is a Gothic masterpiece

a splendid room that witnessed the first meeting of the States General, set up in 1464 by the dukes of Burgundy to regulate provincial contributions to the treasury. The vaulted oak ceiling (begun in 1385 and finished in 1402), with its long pendant keystones at the junctions of the arches, is richly decorated in tones of brown, black, maroon and gold, surrounding painted scenes from the New Testament.

The murals, depicting important events in the city's history, were painted by the De Vriendt brothers in 1905 after the original 1410 wall decorations were lost. The small, delicate balcony near the entrance door was for the town pipers and other musicians. The hall is used for civic ceremonies, receptions and weddings. An adjoining room displays old coins, documents and other artefacts relating to the history of Bruges.

To the right of the Stadhuis as you face it is the small gilded entrance to the **Heilig-Bloedbasiliek** (Basilica of the Holy Blood; Apr–Sept 9.30am–noon, 2–6pm; Oct–Mar Thur–Tue 10am–noon, 2–4pm, Wed 10am–noon; charge). Its three-arched facade was completed by 1534, making it a mere youth in comparison with the Stadhuis. Its ornate stone carvings and gilded statues of angels, knights and their ladies stand below two closely adjoining and strangely Islamic-looking towers of great delicacy. The interior of the basilica is divided into two chapels, a 12th-century Romanesque lower chapel and a Gothic upper chapel, providing a dramatic contrast in styles. The lower chapel is a study in shadows, with austere, unadorned lines, uncompromising Romanesque pillars, and little decoration except for a relief carving over an interior doorway depicting the baptism of St Basil (an early Church Father). St Basil's relics were brought back from Palestine by Robert II, count of Flanders. The faded carving is child-like in style, its naivety emphasised by the two mismatched columns supporting it.

Access to the upper chapel is through a beautiful late Gothic doorway. Ascending by a broad, elegant 16th-century spiral staircase, you can enter the upper chapel beneath the organ case. The lines of the chapel have been spoiled somewhat by over-enthusiastic 19th-century

## Ascension Day

On Ascension Day every year, the holy relic is carried through Bruges in the famous Heilig-Bloed Processie (Procession of the Holy Blood), the most important of West Flanders' festivals. The venerated phial is transported in a flamboyant gold and silver reliquary that is normally kept in the treasury off the chapel.

decoration and murals, but the greater impression is of warmth and richness. The ceiling looks like an upturned boat and the room is flooded with a golden light. The bronze-coloured pulpit is a curious sight, bearing a remarkable resemblance to a cored and stuffed tomato.

In a small side chapel you will find the holy relic from which the church derives its name. Flemish knight Dirk of Alsace returned from the Second Crusade in the Holy Land in 1149 and is said to have brought with him a crystal phial believed to contain some drops of Christ's blood. Once venerated all over medieval Europe, it is still

The Basilica of the Holy Blood is home to a venerated relic

brought out each Friday for the faithful. The dried blood turned to liquid at regular intervals for many years, an event declared by Pope Clement V to be a miracle. The phial is stored in a richly and rather heavily ornate silver tabernacle presented by the archdukes of Spain in 1611. It is carried in procession through the streets every year on Ascension Day.

Opposite the basilica, the **Landhuis van het Brugse Vrije** (Liberty of Bruges Palace) is an early 18th-century neoclassical building on the site of an older structure that usd to house the law courts. (At the rear of the building overlooking the canal are the remains of an attractive 16th-century facade.)

Part of the palatial building now houses the **Bruggemu-seum-Brugse Vrije** (Bruges Museum-Liberty of Bruges; daily 9.30am–12.30pm, 1.30–5pm; charge), with an entrance at Burg 11. The museum has one main exhibit, the **Renais-sancezaal** (Renaissance Hall), the Liberty's restored council chamber. The great black marble and oak Renaissance 'Em-peror Charles' chimneypiece, designed by the painter Lanceloot Blondeel in tribute to Charles V, was started in 1528 and finished in 1531. This is one of the most memo-rable artworks in Bruges: the carving is on a monumental scale, covering an entire wall and joining the ceiling with carved tendrils and caskets. A statue of Charles in full ar-mour, wearing the emblem of the Order of the Golden Fleece, is in the centre. Forty-six coats of arms and ribbons of wood also appear on it. Among many of the scenes, the design de-picts the defeat of the French at Pavia and the biblical story of Susanna and the Elders. The intricate craftsmanship of the piece is superb and quite overwhelming, but the handholds for gentlemen to use while drying their boots are the sort of domestic touch everyone remembers.

Adjoining this building is the statue-laden, Renaissance-style **Oude Civiele Griffie** (Old Registrar's House), com-pleted in 1537. Note how the sinuously curved and scrolled gables contrast with the older, linear step gables of most of the architecture you will see in Bruges.

## Around Vismarkt

Wander through the Renaissance arch joining the Oude Civiele Griffie and the Stadhuis, and follow Blinde Ezelstraat (Blind Donkey Street) across the bridge until you reach the colon-naded **Vismarkt** (Fishmarket; Tue–Sat 8am–1pm). Built in 1821, the market sells fresh fish from the North Sea along with a variety of craft items. Lining both sides of the canal are some pretty little streets.

At Groene Rei (left at the bridge) is the 1634 **Godshuis De Pelikaanhuis** (Pelican House). Easily identified by its Pelican emblem over the doorway, this was once a hospital or almshouse. Such almshouses can be found all over Bruges: they were built by the guilds of the city and wealthy merchants to shelter the sick, elderly and poor. They are usually low, whitewashed cottages like the ones in Zwarte-Leertouwerstraat (take the last right turn in Groene Rei).

Back behind the Vismarkt, you can wander through Huidenvettersplein (Tanners' Square), which has become something of a growth area

Canal cruises are an ideal way to view the city

for cafés and restaurants. The turreted **Huidevettershuis** (Tanners' Guild Hall), built in 1630, is now a restaurant.

Beyond the square, **Rozenhoedkaai** (Rosary Quay) is one of the places from where boat tours depart; do stop to enjoy the view from the quay. The River Dijver – a branch of the Reie – begins at **Sint-Jan Nepomucenusbrug** (St John of Nepomuk Bridge). A statue portrays the good man himself, appropriately the patron saint of bridges. The tree-lined bank of the river – site of a weekend antiques market – passes superb old houses and crosses the canal into Gruuthusestraat. On the left is a complex of museums: the Groeninge, the Brangwyn and the Gruuthuse.

See the best of the Flemish Primitives in the Groeninge Museum

## The Groeninge Museum

**4** The **Groeningemuseum** (Tue–Sun 9.30am–5pm; charge)
contains some of the great works of the Flemish Primitives,
including Van Eyck's portrait of his supercilious-looking
wife Margareta, which is so typical of the painter's in-
credible realism; and Bosch's deeply disturbing *Last Judgement*, with the fires of hell ablaze. The *Judgement of
Cambyses*, painted by Gerard David in 1498, depicts the
judicial skinning of a corrupt judge while detached on-
lookers coolly observe the proceedings.

Other treasures include Memling's glorious *Moreel Tryptych* depicting St Christopher, with portraits in the side
panels, and his *St John Altarpiece*. In addition, there are
magnificent portraits by Hugo van der Goes, Rogier van
der Weyden and Petrus Christus, as well as paintings by
unknown masters, many of them depicting detailed views
of the city.

However, the greatest work in the museum is Van Eyck's *Madonna with Canon George van der Paele*, where the textures and folds of the clothing and carpets are reproduced with breathtaking effect. There is also work from later periods, including a landscape by James Ensor, enigmatic work by René Magritte, and some more recently acquired Flemish Expressionists – but the early Flemish artists steal the show.

## The Arentshuis

The **Arentshuis** (Tue–Sun 9.30am–5pm; charge) at number 16 contains the extensive art collection of Sir Frank Brangwyn, a Welsh artist born in Bruges in 1867 who bequeathed his work to the city when he died in 1956. In addition to his realistic paintings depicting industrial life in the docks and factories, Brangwyn was known for colourful travel scenes. Also on display are items of furniture, prints and rugs that he designed. Temporary exhibitions are held on the ground floor.

## The Gruuthuse Museum

In the courtyard at the rear of the Arentshuis you can see Rik Poot's sculptures of the *Four Horsemen of the Apocalypse*, a scary combination of robotic armour and animal skeletons. A hump-backed bridge connects the courtyard to the **Gruuthuse Bruggemuseum** (Tue–Sun 9.30am–5pm; charge), so called because the original owners had rights to tax the *gruut* used by brewers (the herbs, spices and plants used in brewing before the introduction of hops).

The building itself is one of the museum's best exhibits – a splendid mansion of red brick. Built in the 15th century, it has twice

### Welsh war artist

Frank Brangwyn was a disciple of the Arts and Crafts Movement and apprentice to its greatest exponent, William Morris, before becoming a war artist in World War I.

sheltered fugitive English kings: both Edward IV and Charles II stayed here, in 1471 and 1656 respectively. Inside the house, beautifully furnished in a variety of period styles, there is an evocative smell of polished wood.

The museum has an exceptional collection of lacework, tapestries and musical instruments, including a delicate spinet. Items are labelled in Dutch only, but you do not need labels to admire the imposing medieval kitchen or the magnificent fireplace and beamed ceiling in Room 1. Room 5, with painted angels sculpted in the ceiling beams, provides some interesting views over the rooftops and into the courtyard. There are also fine antique crossbows and a guillotine on display. Finally, the oratory (private chapel) overlooks the chancel of the adjoining Church of Our Lady.

## Onze-Lieve-Vrouwekerk

**6** The exterior of **Onze-Lieve-Vrouwekerk** (Church of Our Lady) is a hodge-podge of different styles and is slightly forbidding. More interesting is the interior, which is filled with religious artworks and treasures (Tue–Fri 9.30am–5pm, Sat 9.30am–4.45pm, Sun 1.30–5pm; charge for parts of the church). Chief among them is the *Madonna and Child* (1504) by Michelangelo, originally intended for Siena Cathedral and the only one of his works to travel outside Italy during his lifetime. It was brought to Bruges by a Flemish merchant, Jan van Moeskroen. The Madonna is a subdued, preoccupied figure, while the infant leans nonchalantly on her knee.

There are some fine paintings here by Pieter Pourbus (*Last Supper* and *Adoration of the Shepherds*) and Gerard David (*Transfiguration*),

### Inland lighthouse

The 122m (400ft) brick tower of Onze-Lieve-Vrouwekerk (the second highest in Belgium) once served as a kind of inland lighthouse for ships on their way to Bruges.

but, after the Michelangelo, it is the chancel area that holds most interest. Here you can see the **tombs** of Charles the Bold and his daughter Mary of Burgundy, fine examples of, respectively, Renaissance and late Gothic carving. Both are richly decorated with coats of arms linked with floral motifs in copper-gilt gold, reds and blues; the figures themselves (with domestic details like the pet dogs at Mary's feet) are also in copper gilt. Whether or not Charles and Mary are actually buried here is a matter of some dispute. Charles died in battle in Nancy in 1477 and it was difficult to identify the body. Mary (who died in a riding accident at the age of 25, bringing to a close the 100-year reign of the House of Burgundy) may be buried among a group of poly-chromed tombs in the choir that were discovered in 1979. You can see the frescoed tombs through windows in the floor and mirrors in front of the sarcophagi.

Michelangelo's *Madonna and Child* in Onze-Lieve-Vrouwekerk

Elsewhere in the church, you'll find the funerary chapel of Pieter Lanchals *(see page 41)*, containing frescoed tombs in maroon and black; and Van Dyck's starkly atmospheric painting of Christ on the Cross. The splendid wooden gallery overlooking the chancel belongs to the adjacent Gruuthuse mansion *(see page 35)* and dates from the 15th century.

## Sint-Janshospitaal

**7** Opposite the church is **Sint-Janshospitaal** (St John's Hospital). Constructed in the 12th century, and now below street level, this is the oldest building in Bruges. In what were once the hospital wards there is an exhibition of historical documents and alarming surgical instruments. The 17th-century pharmacy has a carved relief showing patients sleeping two to a bed. The hospital was still functioning in the 19th century, and there is a strong sense of tradition, enhanced by an informative visitor centre.

## The Memling Museum

**8** Housed in the old hospital church, **Memling in Sint-Jan** (Tue–Sun 9.30am–5pm; charge) is largely devoted to six masterpieces by the Flemish master Hans Memling. The museum is small but is highly recommended. Each of the exhibited works displays Memling's captivating attention to detail and mastery of realism. It's impossible to pick the 'best', but probably the most famous is the detailed *Reliquary of St Ursula*, one of the greatest art treasures in the country. Commissioned by two sisters who worked in the church, the reliquary is in the form of a miniature Gothic chapel with Memling's painted panels in the positions of the windows.

The *Mystic Marriage of St Catherine* includes St John the Evangelist and St John the Baptist, patron saints of the hospital: it has been suggested that saints Catherine and Barbara are portraits of Mary of Burgundy and Margaret of York. A painting by Jan Beerbloch depicts the relaxed standards of hospital hygiene: nurses sweep the floors while dogs wander the wards.

## Around Mariastraat

If you head south along Mariastraat and look left along Nieuwe Gentweg, there are some typical white almshouses that have gardens open to the public. The next turning on the right is Walstraat, a peaceful street of delightful 16th-and 17th-century gabled houses where lacemaking is still practised (outside on warm days).

If your thirst for culture is overtaken by a thirst for something else, a short stroll will bring you to **Brouwerij De Halve Maan** (www.halvemaan.be; Apr–Oct Mon–Fri guided tours hourly 11am–4pm, Sat–Sun until 5pm, Nov–Mar Mon–Fri 11am–3pm, Sat–Sun until 4pm; charge) at Walplein 26. Belgium is well known for its many hundreds of beers, and Bruges beers are exceptionally good. De Halve Maan (The Half Moon) has been brewing in the city since 1564 and today produces a light, highly fermented local beer called Straffe Hendrik (Strong Henry, after its high alcohol content). Brugse Zot beer joined it in 2005. The 45-minute tour of the museum will reveal how it is done, and includes an ascent to the roof for a good view over the gables of central Bruges. The building is suffused with a sweet smell from the brewing process. At the end of the visit, each visitor gets a drink in the congenial bar, lined with every conceivable shape of beer bottle.

The canal frontage of
Sint-Janshospitaal

## The Begijnhof

South of the church along Mariastraat, follow the signposts to the **Begijnhof**.

A nun in the Begijnhof

Belgium is famous for the number of residences for tertiary religious orders, which were for unmarried or widowed women (known as Beguines) who wished to live under religious rule without having to commit themselves to the full vows of a nun. The women cared for the sick and made a living by lacemaking.

The **Prinselijk Begijnhof ten Wijngaarde** (Princely Beguinage of the Vineyard) was founded in 1245 by Margaret of Constantinople and remained a Beguine residence until very recently – it is now a Benedictine convent. Nuns wear the traditional clothes of the Beguines and maintain some of their predecessors' customs. The convent is one of the most attractive Beguine residences. Reached by a bridge over the canal and through an arch, it comprises a circle of white, 17th-century houses set around a courtyard of grass and trees that comes alive with daffodils each spring. In a city replete with picturesque views, this is one of the most photographed places in Bruges. You can visit the Begijnhof's church, **Onze-Lieve-Vrouw van Troost van Spermalie** (Our Lady of Consolation of Spermalie), when the nuns are having a service. Or visit the **Begijnhuisje** (Beguine House; daily Apr–Sept 10am–noon, 1.45–5.30pm, Oct–Nov and Mar 10.30am–noon, 1.45–5pm, Dec–Feb Wed–Thur, Sat–Sun 2.45–4.15pm, Fri 1.45–6pm; charge), one of the Beguines' cottages, still largely in its 17th-century condition. A stroll around the tree-shaded cloister garden, a blaze of colour in spring and summer, is a delight.

Around the Begijnhof the street layout is as it was in the 17th century, so take time to wander around and enjoy the views. This is also where the hard-working carriage horses of Bruges stop to enjoy a well-earned rest mid-tour, with a drink of water pumped from a horse's head statue.

## Minnewater

The picturesque and understandably popular park and lake of **Minnewater** (Lake of Love) lie to the south of Walplein and Wijngaardplein. The lake was originally the inner harbour of Bruges, before the Zwin inlet silted up and cut off the city from the sea; you can still see the 15th-century Sashuis (Lock House). Beyond the Sashuis, the tower on the right is the Poertoren (Powder Tower), a remnant of old fortifications. On the east side of the basin is leafy **Minnewater Park** in which stands **Kasteel Minnewater** (Minnewater Castle), currently empty and awaiting a buyer.

Take Wijngaardstraat and turn right into Noordstraat, to the **Godshuis de Vos** (1713). You can look over the wall into the courtyard of this enchanting almshouse, where the original eight little houses are now converted to six.

## Katelijnestraat

Turn left into Arsenalstraat and left again into Katelijnestraat, to the **Stedelijke Academie voor Schone Kunsten**

### Why the swans?

The presence of swans on Minnewater, so the story goes, stems from the time in 1488 when Emperor Maximilian was imprisoned in Bruges and his councillor, Pieter Lanchals, was beheaded. Lanchals' coat of arms featured a swan, and the emperor ordered that swans be kept on the canals of Bruges for evermore, as a reminder of the city's dreadful crime.

(Municipal Fine Arts Academy), housed in a former Beghard Monastery at No. 86. These male counterparts to the beguines established themselves here in the 13th century. The complex became a school for poor children in 1513 and took on its present role in 1891. Also in Katelijnestraat, at No. **⓫** 43, is the **Diamantmuseum Brugge** (Bruges Diamond Museum; www.diamondmuseum.be; daily 10.30am–5.30pm; charge). The museum documents the history of diamond polishing – a technique thought to have been invented by the Bruges goldsmith, Lodewijk van Berquem, in the mid-15th century. There is a reconstruction of van Berquem's workshop, examples of tools and machinery used in diamond polishing, plus models, paintings and rare rock samples. Daily demonstrations (at 12.15pm) further illustrate the technique.

Katelijnestraat connects with Nieuwe Gentweg, where you can visit a cluster of attractive *godshuizen* (almshouses): **De**

The 'Lake of Love' – picturesque Minnewater

**Meulenaere** (dating from 1613); **Sint-Jozef** (St Joseph; 1674); and, around the corner in Drie Kroezenstraat, **Onze-Lieve-Vrouw van de Zeven Weeën** (Our Lady of the Seven Sorrows founded in 1654).

## WEST FROM THE MARKT

Go along Steenstraat, a beautiful street lined with gabled guild houses, headquarters of the trading and craft guilds that contributed so much to the medieval city's life. There is the Bakers' Guild House at No. 19, the Stonemasons' Guild House at No. 25, the Joiners' Guild House at No. 38, and the Shoemakers' Guild House at No. 40. All of these now house either shops or banks. This brings you to **Simon Stevinplein**, and its bronze sculpture of the Bruges mathematician and scientist Simon Stevin, who fled from his native city around 1580 during the anti-Protestant persecutions carried out by its Spanish rulers. He later lived and worked in Holland. The square was laid out in 1819 and the statue, which depicts Stevin holding a set of dividers in one hand and a manuscript in the other, dates from 1847.

If you make a short detour south of Simon Stevinplein to Oude Burg, you will find the **Hof van Watervliet**. The 16th-century buildings have been much restored, but are still of interest. Former residents included the humanist scholar Erasmus and the exiled Charles II of England.

Further along Steenstraat you will come to **Sint-Salvatorskathedraal** (Holy Saviour's Cathedral; www.sintsalvator.be; Mon 2–5.45pm, Tue–Fri 8.30–11.45am, 2–5.45pm, Sat 8.30–11.45am, 2–3.30pm, Sun 9–10.15am, 2–5pm; worshippers only during services; free, charge for museum). The oldest parish church in Bruges, it has been a cathedral since 1834, replacing the city centre cathedral destroyed by the French in the late 18th century. Parts of the building date from the

**Concertgebouw**

'T Zand Square was chosen as the site of the city's concert hall, Concertgebouw Brugge, the main focus of Bruges' year as European City of Culture in 2002.

12th and 13th centuries, though the church was originally founded in the 10th century. The Gothic interior is quite spartan and curiously unfocused in design, but the choir stalls and the Baroque rood screen showing God the Father are worth a look. The cathedral has its own museum, located off the right transept. Specialising in liturgical objects, it is worth visiting for its Flemish paintings, including work by Dirk Bouts and Pieter Pourbus.

## Around 't Zand Square

Continuing along Zuidzandstraat, you come to bustling **'t Zand**, a square lined with numerous hotels and cafés. Notice the fountain and groups of modern sculpture by Stefaan Depuydt and Livia Canestraro. The four female figures in *Bathing Women* symbolise Antwerp, Bruges, Kortrijk and Ghent; *Landscape of Flanders* is an abstract representation of the region's flat terrain; *The Cyclists* is an expression of youth and hope for the future; and *The Fishermen* represents Bruges' ancient ties with the sea.

Along Boeveriestraat from 't Zand, at Klokstraat, is the **Kapucijnenkerk** (Capuchin Church), the church of a Capuchin monastery built here in 1869 to replace an earlier one in what is now 't Zand Square. The monastery was demolished to make way for the city's original railway station, which has itself vanished. On the left side of Boeveriestraat stands the Benedictine **Sint-Godelieve Abdij** (St Godelina Abbey); the nuns first moved into the city in the 16th century and established themselves here in 1623. Behind its brick facade is a wide green lawn. Across the street, you will find the grounded **Dumery-Klok** (Dumery Bell). This used to hang in the belfry above the Markt and was placed here as a memento of the 18th-century Dumery Bell Foundry that once stood here. Also on this street and around the neighbourhood are the *godshuizen* (almshouses) **Van Campen** (1436), **Van Peenen** (1621), **Gloribus** (1634), **Sucx** (1436), and **De Moor** (1480).

The park that now occupies the line of the city's medieval wall and moat leads north, past the **Oud Waterhuis** (Old Water House; 1394), part of the city's water distribution system, which drew supplies from the canals and other sources. Continuing north brings you to the **Smedenpoort** (Marshal's Gate), one of the four fortified city gates that survive of the nine that were once dotted around the now mostly vanished city walls. Dating from 1368 with additions from the 17th century, it is a powerful-looking piece of military engineering.

*The Cyclists*, in 't Zand Square

Take Smedenstraat back towards 't Zand and the Markt. A short diversion into Kreupelenstraat lets you visit the **Onze-Lieve-Vrouw-van-Blindekenskapel** (Chapel of Our Lady of the Blind). This bright and simple 17th-century church has a carved pulpit from 1659 and a gilded 14th-century statue of the *Madonna and Child* above a side altar. Every 15 August, on the feast of the Assumption, a procession leaves from here and wends its way to the church of Onze-Lieve-Vrouw van de Potterie (Our Lady of the Pottery) in the northeast of the city (see page 55). A further diversion, this time along the handsome Speelmansrei canal, leads to the little Gothic **Speelmanskapel** (Minstrels' Church; 1421). The nearby **Stadspark Sebrechts** stands on land once occupied by the nuns of the Sint-Elisabethklooster, which was dissolved in 1784. In summer the park becomes an open-air museum of modern sculpture.

The imposing Prinsenhof

Nearby Noordzandstraat is the site of the **Prinsenhof** (Prince's Court), once the residence of dukes and duchesses of Burgundy, and later of Habsburg emperors and empresses. During the Burgundian period it was the ultimate in pomp and splendour. When Charles the Bold was engaged in his ill-starred quest to make Burgundy a third continental power, alongside France and Germany, the Prinsenhof was a radiant nucleus, and Bruges the largest, richest and most powerful city north of the Alps. Burgundian-era highlights took place in this setting. Philip the Good celebrated his marriage to Isabella of Portugal in 1430 and Charles the Bold his marriage to Margaret of York in 1468 with banquets that made the term 'Burgundian' a byword for lavishness. Duchess Mary gave birth to Philip the Handsome here in 1479, and in 1482 she died here, as had Philip the Good in 1467.

Not much survives of the 14th-century palace, yet the Prinsenhof is still imposing. Remodelled constantly through the Burgundian century, the palace was put up for sale in 1631 and purchased in 1662 by the Order of St Francis, for a convent. In 1794, the nuns departed for Delft, ahead of the incoming French Revolutionary army, and the property was sold again. In 1888, nuns were back, this time the French Dames de la Retraite. A century later it was sold to a private concern and used as a centre for exhibitions, conferences and concerts. It now houses the Kempinski Hotel Dukes' Palace.

> **Golden Fleece**
>
> Philip the Good founded the chivalric Order of the Golden Fleece in 1430, on the occasion of his wedding to Isabella of Portugal. Its knights formed the cream of Burgundian high society, but according to a French report published in 1620, the Golden Fleece referred not to the mythological quest of Jason and the Argonauts, but to the lustrous hair of one of Philip's mistresses.

In little Muntplein square is a small equestrian statue, **Flandria Nostra**, of Mary of Burgundy riding side-saddle. The daughter of Charles the Bold, she died in 1482 at age 25 after falling from her horse while hunting, and now occupies a sarcophagus in the Church of Our Lady *(see page 37)*. Just before re-entering the Markt, at Geldmuntstraat 9, you pass the Art Nouveau shop front of the **De Medici Sorbetière.**

## NORTH FROM THE MARKT

The city north of the Markt used to be the home and business premises of the merchants of medieval Bruges, for it was common practice to live and work in the same building. The avenues of elegant houses from this period are punctuated with grandiose mansions dating from the 18th century, and the canals here meet and diverge in broad highways of water – it is no wonder many visitors regard this as their favourite section of the city.

### Jan van Eyckplein

Just a few minutes' walk north from the Markt along Vlamingstraat is **Jan van Eyckplein** and adjoining Spiegelrei. Bruges has many former harbours, and this one was the busiest of them all; the canal that terminates here once extended as far as the Markt. It was also the commercial and diplomatic centre for medieval Bruges, and foreign consulates opened along the length of Spiegelrei.

There is a statue of the painter in the square, but it is the buildings that really stand out. Jan looks directly at the most striking of these, the **Poortersloge** (Burghers' Lodge; 1417). The pencil tower may point heavenwards, but the building was in fact the meeting place of the wealthier city merchants. On its facade is a statue of the jolly bear that features in the city's coat of arms. It was also the emblem of a jousting club that held its events in the marketplace outside. The restored building now houses the Bruges State Archives.

To the right of the Poortersloge is the 15th-century **Tol-huis** (Customs House), where tolls were levied by (among others over the years) the dukes of Luxembourg, whose coat of arms is on the facade. This fine Gothic building now holds the library and documentation centre of West Flanders.

Adjacent Spanjaardstraat was the centre of the city's Spanish mercantile community in the 16th century and the many mansions in this area testify to their wealth. Among the best, at No. 16, is **Huis De la Torre** (*c.*1500), with an ornately decorated Gothic facade and a mid-16th-century Renaissance portal. Ignatius de Loyola, the Spanish priest who founded the Jesuit Order, was a frequent guest in the house at No. 9.

## East of Jan van Eyckplein

From Jan van Eyckplein you can wander through the lovely canalside street of Spinolarei into Koningstraat and Sint-Maartensplein, where you will find **Sint-Walburgakerk** (Church of St Walpurga). This impressive Baroque church was built in 1643 by the Bruges Jesuit Pieter Huyssens, with a statue of St Francis Xavier standing above the entrance door.

Jan van Eyck looks down on the square that bears his name

The Baroque interior is for the most part unremarkable, except for the fabulous pulpit by Artus Quellin the Younger, which has twin stairways and a scalloped canopy uplifted by trumpeting angels.

Crossing the canal and following Sint-Annarei south into Sint-Annakerkstraat, you will see the slender spire of **Sint-Annakerk** (Church of St Anne), a 1624 Baroque replacement for the Gothic church demolished in 1561. Inside, the carving of the rood screen, confessionals and pulpit, as well as the rich panelling, are well worth viewing if the church is open.

The unusual tower with the vaguely Oriental look visible from Sint-Annakerk belongs to the **Jeruzalemkerk** (Jerusalem Church; Mon–Sat 10am–5pm; shared charge with Kantcentrum, *see next page*), in Peperstraat. The church is named after and modelled on the Church of the Holy Sepulchre in Jerusalem. Dating from 1428, it was built by the Adornes family, originally merchants from Genoa, who had travelled on a pilgrimage to Jerusalem and were so impressed by the church that they built this one in Bruges. There is even a copy of Christ's memorial tomb in the crypt.

Skulls and bones adorn the altar of the Jeruzalemkerk

It is a sombre, stark place with very good examples of 15th- and 16th-century stained glass, some of which depicts members of the Adornes family. In the nave you can see effigies of Anselmus Adornes and his wife. The altar is carved in a rather macabre fashion, with skulls and bones, and the cave-like atmosphere of the church is emphasised by the space behind the altar and above the crypt, which rises almost to the full height of the tower to create an eerie, artificial-looking cavern.

Beside Jeruzalemkerk is the **Kantcentrum** (Lace Centre; www.kancentrum.eu; Mon–Sat 10am–5pm; shared charge with Jeruzalemkerk), a museum and workshop in the 15th-century Jeruzalem-godshuizen (almshouses) founded by the Adornes family. Fine examples of the craft of lacemaking and demonstrations by the workers and their students can be seen.

A sign points down Balstraat towards the **Bruggemuseum Volkskunde** (Folklore Museum; Tue–Sun 9.30am–5pm; charge), at Rolweg 40, housed in a delightful row of 17th-century whitewashed almshouses built by the cobblers' guild, and the life of everyday West Flanders is recreated in the traditionally furnished interiors, including a primary school class, coopers' and milliners' workshops, a sweet shop and every-

## Lacemaking

Lacemaking by hand in Bruges, an industry which at its peak in the 1840s provided steady employment – and low wages – for 10,000 local women and girls, is making a slow but steady comeback, thanks mainly to the demand from visiting tourists. Even in its heyday, lacemaking was a cottage industry. Handmade lace is expensive, and most of the items sold in the city's multitude of lace shops today is machine-made and often imported.

The most popular kind of lace made in Bruges is bobbin lace, which is created using a technique developed in Flanders in the 16th century. Threads of silk, linen or cotton on as many as 700 different bobbins are crossed and braided around a framework of pins. It takes great skill and concentration to do this and it is fascinating to watch an experienced craftswoman (it generally is a woman) at work. Other styles of handmade Belgian lace are *bloemenwerk* (flower lace), *rozenkant* (pearled rosary) and *toveressesteek* (fairy stitch).

day household scenes. A traditional ale house – De Zwarte Kat (The Black Cat) – offers respite for the weary walker.

Cross Rolweg into Carmersstraat and turn right to pass the **Engels Klooster Onze-Lieve-Vrouw van Nazareth** (English Convent of Our Lady of Nazareth) at No. 85, founded in 1629 by an order of English Ursuline nuns, with a domed church (1739). The last words of the Flemish poet-priest Guido Gezelle *(see below)*, who died here in 1899, are carved on the facade: '... and I was so happy to hear the birds sing'.

**17** ▷    Further up Carmersstraat is the lodge of the **Sint-Sebasti-aansgilde** (St Sebastian's Guild; www.sebastiaansgilde.be; Apr–Sept Tue–Thur 10am–noon, Sat 2–5pm, Oct–Mar Tue–Thur and Sat 2–5pm; charge). The guild of archers was a powerful, wealthy and influential force in the city, and its sumptuous quarters (16th–17th centuries) reflect this. Inside is a collection of arms and accoutrements, furnishings, gold and silver plate, paintings and other works of art. Among the guild's past members have been Belgian royalty, and England's King Charles II – who paid for the banqueting hall – and his brother Henry, both then in exile in Bruges. A portrait of Henry hangs above the fireplace.

Turn right into Kruisvest, where you will see, overlooking the canal, the **Sint-Janshuismolen** (St John's House Wind-mill; 1770). Then go right again into Rolweg, where at No. 64 stands the **Bruggemuseum-Gezelle** (Tue–Sun 9.30am–12.30pm, 1.30–5pm; charge), dedicated to the poet-priest Guido Gezelle (1830–99), in the house where he was born. Surrounded by a large garden, the brick-built, rather gloomy house contains objects related to Gezelle's life and work, in-cluding copies of manuscripts and editions of his poetry.

Return to Kruisvest and pass the **Bonne-Chièremolen**, a wooden stilt-windmill, then go right into Stijn Streuvelsstraat. At No. 59 is the lodge of the **Sint-Jorisgilde** (St George's Guild; open on request; charge). Unlike the archers of St Sebastian's Guild, St George's members were crossbowmen. Their ornate guild house contains a fine collection of crossbows and the guild's archives. In the garden is a vertical target-mast and walkways protected from descending arrows.

## West of Jan van Eyckplein

If you return to Jan van Eyckplein you can follow Acadamiestraat from the west side of the square. It joins Grauwwerkersstraat, where at No. 35 you find the elegant **Huis Ter Beurze**. Now serving as a centre for conferences, receptions and exhibitions, the 15th-century house belonged to the Van der Beurze family. They leased rooms to city merchants, who lived and worked in the house; the family's name (rendered as 'bourse' or 'beurs') has co buildingme to designate the place for a commercial stock exchange in many languages.

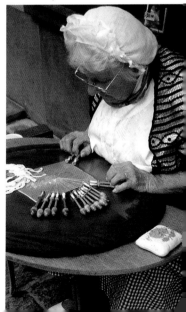

Lace is still made the traditional way at the Kantcentrum

The Genoese merchants in Bruges did their business in the adjacent building. Genuese Loge (Genoese Lodge). The building, dating from 1441, now houses the **Frietmuseum** (Fries Museum; www.frietmuseum.be; daily 10am–5pm; charge), dedicated to the humble but tasty – and somewhat misleadingly named – 'French' fries, or chips.

North of the Markt, there are no grand churches to compare with Onze-Lieve-Vrouwekerk or Sint-Salvatorskathedraal, but **Sint-Jakobskerk** (St James's Church; Apr–Sept Mon–Sat 10am–noon, 2–5pm, Sun 2–5pm; worshippers only during services; charge) in Sint-Jakobsstraat makes the most determined bid for grandiosity. Thanks to generous gifts from the dukes of Burgundy, the 13th-century Gothic church was improved and enlarged to its present size. It has a pleasing internal harmony strangely lacking in many of the other churches in Bruges, and is illuminated by a pale pink light when the sun is shining. The interior is decorated with an abundance of 16th–18th-century paintings and tombs.

The glorious canopied pulpit is worth a closer inspection for its intricate, skilful carving. Among the most interesting of the tombs is the two-tiered arrangement of Ferry de Gros and his two wives. De Gros, who died in 1544, was a treasurer of the Order of the Golden Fleece. The tomb is reminiscent of the Italian Renaissance, with ornate floral designs on the ceramic wall-tiles. A walk of less than 1km (½ mile) along Ezelstraat leads past the 15th-century **Karmelietenkerk** (Carmelite Church) with its gloomy Baroque interior, to the **Ezelpoort** (Donkey Gate), or **Sint-Jacobspoort** (St James's Gate). One of the four surviving gates of the nine that once allowed passage through the 14th-century city walls, this formidable-looking bastion dates from 1370 and has been rebuilt several times.

## North of Jan van Eyckplein

Connected to Woensdagmarkt and Oosterlingenplein is Krom Genthof, a small square on which stands the **Oosterlingenhuis** (Easterners' House; 1481), once the local headquarters of the Hanseatic League, which was trading with Bruges as early as the 13th century. Part of the house survives in what is now the Hotel Bryghia.

Now walk across the canal bridge into Potterierei and a different world from the busy city centre, for an insight into everyday Bruges. Simply enjoy the canalside houses, the canal views and bridges, and the peace and quiet. Near the far end of Potterierei a wooden gateway marks the entrance to the **Duinenabdij** (Abbey of the Dunes), a foundation that was based at Koksijde on the North Sea coast until it was forced to retreat from encroaching seas in 1560, and in the 17th century set up here. Since 1833 this has been the Episcopal Seminary.

Continue up Potterierei to No. 78–9, **Onze-Lieve-Vrouw** ◀ ⑲ **ter Potterie** (Our Lady of the Pottery; museum Tue–Sun 9.30am–12.30pm, 1.30–5pm; charge), formerly a hospice, with a recorded history going back to 1276. Most of the complex is now a senior citizens' home, but part of it – including a ward and cloisters dating from the 14th to the 15th centuries – has been opened as a museum, displaying tapestries, furniture from the 15th–17th centuries, silverware, religious objects and books, and early Flemish paintings. The adjoining 14th-century church, which used to be the Potters' Guild chapel, is a little gem, with a Baroque interior containing, among other treasures, a 13th-century statue of Our Lady of the Pottery said to have miraculous powers; and a 16th-century tapestry of the Nativity.

Huge Sint-Jakobskerk looks down on Sint-Jakobsstraat

Return along Potterierei to the first bridge, a drawbridge, cross over to Langerei, and keep going south. Turn right into Sint-Gilliskoorstraat, to the **Sint-Gilliskerk** (St Giles' Church), built around 1241 in the early Gothic style, but drastically altered in the 15th century, leaving it with three aisles in place of the earlier cruciform shape. Among the treasures inside are a superb organ and a cycle of paintings from 1774 by Bruges artist Jan Garemijn, depicting the history of the Trinitarian Brothers. The artist Hans Memling was buried here in 1494.

## TRIPS FROM BRUGES

After the near perfection of Bruges, any other town in the region can seem disappointing, but there are several places of interest that you may like to explore on your way to or from the city. Most of them are no more than a few miles from

A paddle boat moored by Damme's windmill

Bruges. The exceptions are Ghent, the World War I battlefields around Ypres (Ieper), and Veurne. For descriptions of Brussels, Antwerp and Belgium's coastal resorts, see the *Berlitz Pocket Guide to Brussels* and the *Berlitz Pocket Guide to Belgium*.

## Damme

The attractive roads leading to this picturesque village, 7km (4 miles) northeast of Bruges, are lined with pollarded trees, all kinked in exactly the same spot by the prevailing wind that blows across the open countryside. Once the outer port of its larger neighbour, **Damme** still retains an air of medieval prosperity, with some fine old buildings and excellent restaurants around its marketplace. With a windmill, and skating on the canal in winter, Damme is the epitome of a typical Flemish village.

**20**

Damme's main street (Kerkstraat) has a delightful **Stadhuis** (Town Hall) built in 1468, with four corner turrets. In front of the building stands a statue of the poet Jacob van Maerlant (1230–96), who wrote his most important works in Damme. The white sandstone facade is adorned with further statues of historic notables including Charles the Bold and Margaret of York. At one corner, two 'stones of justice' hang from the wall. They used to be tied to the neck or feet of unfortunate women who had given offence in some way, and who were then made to parade round the village.

To the right of the building as you face it, is **De Grote Sterre** (The Great Star), a twin-gabled 15th-century house that was the home of the Spanish governor in the 17th century. Almost destroyed in a storm in 1990, it has undergone extensive restoration. It now houses the tourist information office. Four doors further down is the 15th-century house where the wedding party of Charles the Bold and Margaret of York was held in 1468. Royal weddings were celebrated in lavish style: in Bruges the festivities lasted two weeks.

**Sint-Janshospitaal** (St John's Hospital) is across the road and down from the Stadhuis. Founded in 1249, it includes a Baroque chapel and a museum of paintings, liturgical objects and sacred books. Further up the street and visible from the museum is the 13th-century tower of one of Bruges' prominent beacons, the **Onze-Lieve-Vrouwekerk** (Church of Our Lady). The church has endured many vicissitudes down the centuries, including a fire started in 1578 by soldiers of William of Orange. The tower, gaining its present appearance as a result of partial demolition in 1725, is now the haunt of jackdaws. The separate nave, which has been restored, can be visited in the summer, when the site seems less menacing.

Signposts lead you to the town's former herring market, which comprises an attractive circle of whitewashed cottages surrounding the village's first drinking-water pump.

## Dudzele

This village beside the Boudewijn Kanaal to Zeebrugge, just north of Bruges, lies on the route to Lissewege (see below). Pause for a look at the ruined 12th-century Romanesque **tower** at **Sint-Pieters-Bandenkerk** (Church of St Peter in Chains) in the centre. Across the road is a small museum of local history, the **Heemkundigmuseum De Groene Tente** (The Green Tent; Feb–Dec 1st Sun in month 2–6pm; charge).

At Westkapelse Steenweg 1, the **Gallo-Romeinse Wijnkelder** produces mead (honey wine) and holds Gallo-Roman banquets.

### Bruges to Damme

In the summer, you can take a paddle-boat canal cruise from Noorwegse Kaai in Bruges to Damme. Alternatively, take a No. 4 bus from the railway station – or walk or cycle along the canalside paths.

## Lissewege

This pretty village of whitewashed old houses north of Bruges stands along the **Lis-**

**seweegs Vaartje**, a narrow canal that in medieval times connected Lissewege and Bruges. In the main square, Onder de Toren, stands the early Gothic **Onze-Lieve-Vrouw-Bezoekingskerk** (Church of Our Lady of the Visitation), dating from 1225–50, with a flat-topped tower 50m (162ft) high, from which a carillon tune occasionally bursts forth. Inside the church are a superb Baroque organ, 17th- and 18th-century paintings, and a replica of a statue – said to have been miraculous – of the Madonna and Child, destroyed by Dutch Protestants in the 16th century.

## Zeebrugge
A visit to this port and coastal resort – 'Sea Bruges' – should add to your understanding of Bruges. Visit **Seafront Zeebrugge** (www.seafront.be; daily July–Aug 10am–7pm, June and Sept 10am–6pm; charge), a harbour theme park that is

The delightful Stadhuis in Damme

full of interest, especially for children. Among many maritime attractions here are the old West-Hinder lightship; an interactive exhibition on life on, below and beside the sea, and boat tours of the harbour.

## De Haan

**22** ▶ Widely considered the jewel of the Belgian coast, **De Haan** (Le Coq in French) is 16km (10 miles) from Bruges. The central area of De Haan, known as De Concessie (The Concession), is filled with Belle Epoque villas, some converted to hotels and some privately owned. De Haan's tourist office is housed in the 1902 **Tramstation** at Koninklijk Plein, which has Art Nouveau lines and later Art Deco features. Close by are two pagoda-like pavilions, now kiosks, built in 1904 for the town's Casino, which was itself built in 1899 and has since been demolished. The **Hotel Des Brasseurs** is another

### The Coast Tram

Belgium's North Sea coastline stretches 64km (40 miles) from the Dutch to the French border. Access to the entire coast is made easy by the *Kusttram* (Coast Tram), which in two hours runs almost the full length of the shore, between Knokke-Heist and De Panne. It is the world's longest tramline, with 67km (42 miles) of tracks. These pass through chic Knokke-Heist, the busy port of Zeebrugge, the yacht harbour at Blankenberge, Belle Epoque De Haan, bustling Ostend, the fishing harbour of Nieuwpoort and the long beaches of Oostduinkerke and De Panne. For a considerable part of the way the tram runs along just behind the sand dunes; on other stretches it plunges into busy towns like Ostend and Zeebrugge. You can use it either as a touring option or as a straightforward and fast way to get from one place to another. The *Kusttram* is operated by the public transport company of Flanders, De Lijn (tel: 070-22 02 00; www.delijn.be/dekusttram).

Belle Epoque gem with Art Nouveau elements. Facing it is the domed **Grand Hotel Belle Vue**, opened in the 1920s in what was a private villa. In adjacent Rembrandt-laan a cluster of villas dating from 1925–7 are listed as historic monuments.

From Koninklijk Plein, walk north along Leopold-laan past the **Hotel Belle Epoque**, the Art Deco **Hotel Astoria** (1930) and

Riding on the sands at De Haan

the striking **Stadhuis** (Town Hall; 1899), originally the Grand Hôtel du Coq-sur-Mer. In Jean d'Ardennelaan, west of the Town Hall, Albert Einstein lived for six months in 1933 in the **Villa Savoyarde** after fleeing from Nazi Germany. Parallel to Leopoldlaan is Maria Hendrikalaan, where at No. 20 is the **Hotel Atlanta**, formerly Crown Prince Albert's villa (1901).

With its safe waters and golden sands, De Haan is a popular family resort. Part of the beach, which is lined with open-air café terraces, is designated for windsurfing. Just west of the resort, golfers play the 18-hole links course of the **Koninklijke Golf Club Oostende** (Royal Ostend Golf Club), bordered by the **Natuurreservaat De Kijkuit** (De Kijkuit Nature Reserve) and its protected sand dunes.

## Oostende (Ostend)

Belgium's liveliest North Sea resort – the 'Queen of the Coast' – is quickly reached by train from Bruges. Outside **Oostende** railway station stands a reminder of the town's maritime heritage. The green-hulled **IJslandvaarder Amandine** (Iceland

Fishing Boat *Amandine*), built in 1961, ended her Arctic voyaging in 1995. This last of Ostend's Iceland-bound trawlers is now 'moored' permanently at the edge of the harbour, in a dry basin. Adjacent **Visserskaai** (Fishermen's Wharf) is lined with seafood restaurants and seafood stalls. On the harbour side, you can observe fish, shellfish and sea plants in the **Noordzeeaquarium** (North Sea Aquarium; daily Apr–Sept 10am–12.30pm, 2–5pm, Oct–Mar Sat–Sun and holidays 10am–12.30pm, 2–6pm; charge). Close by is the **Vistrap** (Fish Market), where the day's trawler catch is sold.

Post-war apartments line Albert I Promenade, replacing demolished 19th-century mansions on the once-fashionable seafront esplanade. Turn left into Vlaanderenstraat, to the 19th-century **James Ensor Huis** (Wed–Mon 10am–noon, 2–5pm; charge), at No. 27, where the Anglo-Belgian painter lived from 1916 until his death in 1949. In Ensor's time, this undistinguished town house had a souvenir shop on the ground floor and his studio on the first. Continuing beside the beach brings you to the **Casino-Kursaal**, a 1950s replacement for an 1887 original blown up by the Germans in World War II. In addition to gaming tables, there are restaurants and cafés.

You now reach the 19th-century **Venetiaanse Gaanderijen** (Venetian Galleries). At the entrance to this former royal pavilion is a bronze sculpture of King Baudouin (1951–93), on foot and wearing a raincoat, on a visit to Ostend. Albert I Promenade joins the Zeedijk (Sea Dike) as you come face to face with an equestrian statue (dating from 1931) of King Leopold II (1865–1909). Adjacent to this begins the long **Koninklijke Gaanderijen** (Royal Galleries), built in 1906 by French architect Charles Girault so that Leopold II and his court could shelter from the wind as they passed along the seafront. The plush Art Deco Thermae Palace Hotel in the middle dates from 1933.

Now go east on Koningin Astridlaan and Warschauw-straat to Leopold I Plein with an **equestrian statue** of King Leopold I (1831–65). If you are interested in modern art, you could make a long trek south on Rogierlaan, then into Romestraat to the **Kunst Museum aan Zee** (Art Museum by the Sea; Tue–Sun 10am–6pm; charge) at No. 11. In this converted Modernist department store you can see mostly Belgian works by the likes of Panamarenko and Jan Fabre. Take Witte Nonnenstraat to Wapenplein, a square with a wrought-iron bandstand in the middle. On the square's southern rim is the **Oostends Historisch Museum De Plate** (De Plate Ostend Historical Museum; mid June–mid Sept and school holidays Wed–Mon 10am–noon, 2–5pm; mid Sept–mid June Sat 10am–noon, 2–5pm; charge).

At the end of Kerkstraat, the **Sint-Petrus-en-Pauluskerk** (Church of Sts Peter and Paul), a colossal neo-Gothic edifice,

Seaside trinkets for sale

Veurne stands on the junction of several canals

holds the tomb of Belgium's first queen, Marie-Louise of Orléans, who died in Ostend in 1850. Back at the harbour, in Vindictivelaan, the **Jachthaven** (Yacht Harbour) hosts the three-masted schooner **Mercator**, a merchant marine training ship that spends most of its time here as a floating museum.

## Veurne

A small town (with a population not much greater than that of Damme), just 6km (4 miles) from the border with France, **Veurne** grew from a 9th-century fortress and now has an attractive central marketplace, among the best in Belgium. The town's *Boetprocessie* (Procession of the Penitents) takes place on the last Sunday in July, presenting scenes from Christ's Passion. Owing much to Spanish influence (the town once served as a Spanish garrison), the procession is similar to the Spanish celebration of *Semana Santa* (Holy Week). There are also other processions staged during Easter and Lent.

Most of Veurne's places of interest are in or alongside the central Grote Markt, where you will also find plenty of cafés and restaurants. Tickets for guided tours and carriage rides through the town are available in the summer months from the tourist office in the square.

The typical yellow Flemish brick is much in evidence, together with an architectural style that shows the Spanish presence in its restraint. The gabled **Stadhuis** (Town Hall) in the Grote Markt, built in 1612, has an attractive loggia of bluestone contrasting with the yellow brick of the rest of the structure. The building is open to visitors; among its fine interiors are some unusual and impressive leather wall hangings originating from Córdoba in southern Spain.

The **Landhuis**, adjoining the Stadhuis, was built in 1616, its Gothic bell-tower topped with a Baroque spire. Next door is a delightful parade of five houses with step gables, each with a different design of columns around the windows. The cafés on the ground floors spill out into the square on warm days. On the northeast side of the square is the **Spaans Paviljoen** (Spanish Pavilion) which, as the name suggests, was the headquarters for Spanish officers during the 17th century. Across the road, the building with all the window shutters is the Renaissance **Vleeshuis** (Meat Market), built in 1615, and now a library.

The imposing, unfinished tower of **Sint-Niklaaskerk** (Church of St Nicholas), rising from nearby Appelmarkt, can be climbed to get a good view; the 13th-century structure has a carillon. The other church in the town is **Sint-Walburgakerk** (Church of St Walpurga), construction of which began in 1250 with ambitious plans that eventually proved too much for the little town. It has a splendid 27m (90ft) nave. The interior of the church is worth a visit, more for its overall effect than for any specific item, though there is a fine Baroque pulpit.

An ornate museum
sign in Ypres

## Ypres and Flanders Fields

Southwest of Bruges towards the border with France lies **Flanders Fields**, a vast area of countryside that witnessed military carnage on an unprecedented scale. Although the senseless waste of millions of lives in World War I has gone down in history, the staggering numbers killed nevertheless still have the power to shock. Row upon row of gravestones in the many cemeteries of the area testify to the butchery of war. Whether or not you have relatives buried here, the peacefulness of the place and the solidarity in death of troops from all sides make for a moving and strangely comforting experience – the soldiers' ordeal is at an end.

   **Ypres** (Ieper) is a name that still resonates in the collective memory. The focus of repeated attacks and counter-attacks, it was shelled to destruction during World War I, then carefully reconstructed over the next 40 years. Nothing old remains in the bustling town, but it has an open, relaxed central Grote Markt and an imposing Stadhuis. The **In Flanders Fields Museum** (www.inflandersfields.be; Apr–mid-Nov daily 10am–6pm; mid-Nov–Mar Tue–Sun 10am–5pm; charge) is a striking interactive museum located in the reconstructed **Lakenhalle** (Cloth Hall). It uses historical documents, film footage, poetry, song and sound effects to evoke the brutal experience of trench warfare in the Ypres Salient.

The **Menin Gate** memorial, located just off the Grote Markt, is built on a cutting through which thousands of men made their way towards the Ypres Salient. Designed by Reginald Blomfield, it comprises a classical facade fronting a vast arch with three open ceiling oculi. It is inscribed with the names of nearly 55,000 British soldiers who died in battle but have no known graves.

Every evening at 8pm, the Last Post is played here by local volunteer buglers to comemorate those who died. This ceremony has taken place every evening since July 1928, except for the period when the city was occupied by the German army during World War II.

## The War Cemeteries

Just southeast of Ypres, near Zillebeke, on Hill 62 stands a memorial to the Canadian troops who lost their lives. Near the hill, **Sanctuary Wood Cemetery** preserves a few remaining parts of trenches. At Hill 60 a little further beyond Zillebeke, a roadside memorial commemorates the fallen of Australia, behind which lies a field of mounds and hollows, created by intensive bombardment, where you can still make out the ruins of bunkers. This 'strategically important' hill was constantly taken and retaken throughout World War I. Today, sheep graze here and birds sing in the trees.

### Tours of Remembrance

There are coach tours available from Bruges that visit selected towns, war cemeteries and memorials. Alternatively, if you wish to take more time and follow your own inclinations, it is worth taking a car (or even a bicycle) and making use of 'Route 14–18', a signposted route through the battlefield area of the Ypres Salient. It should be stressed, however, that nothing much remains of the battlefields. Where you wish to go will depend on any family connections you may have with the war, and our survey of sites is necessarily selective.

A little over 10km (6 miles) northeast of Ypres, situated
**26** ▶ off the N332 before Passendale (Passchendaele), is **Tyne Cot
Military Cemetery**. Designed by the architect Sir Herbert
Baker, the cemetery was intended to evoke the appearance
of a traditional English graveyard, with white gravestones
standing honourably in regular formation on a neat green
lawn. Its large Cross of Sacrifice in Portland stone is built
on the site of the Tyne Cot dressing station that was finally
captured by Australian troops in 1917. The slight rise on
which the cemetery is located affords a view over the now
peaceful countryside.

The German cemetery located at **Langemark**, approximately 16km (10 miles) north of Ypres, contains the remains
of more than 44,000 German soldiers – over half of them in
a mass grave. It is referred to as the Students' Cemetery because so many young soldiers perished in the Ypres Salient
in 1914 and 1915. The gravestones are simple tablets that
lie flush with the lawn, on ground sheltered by mature trees.
The cemetery contains the remnants of three bunkers.

Further northwest, 4km (2½ miles) outside the town of
Diksmuide, **Vladslo** German cemetery is the site of more
than 25,000 German graves and an extremely moving
memorial sculpture by Käthe Kollwitz (1867–1945) entitled
*Grieving Parents*. The German sculptor's younger son, Peter,
killed in October 1914, lies buried there.

In fact, there are more than 150 war cemeteries in this
area, making it seem as if Flanders Fields belong more to the
dead than to the living.

## Sint-Andries

Two large country estates are embedded in the forests a short
**27** ▶ distance southwest of Bruges, in the city's **Sint-Andries** district. **Domein Beisbroek** has a **Natuurcentrum** (Nature
Centre; Apr–Nov Mon–Fri 2–5pm, Sun 2–6pm, Mar Sun

Tyne Cot is the largest military cemetery in the world

2–6pm; free), a Volkssterrenwacht (Observatory; www.
beisbroek.be; open for pre-arranged groups) and the **Zeiss
Planetarium** (displays Wed and Sun 3pm and 4.30pm, Fri
8.30pm; charge), where you can learn about the mysteries
of the night sky.

At nearby **Domein Tudor** the splendid neo-Gothic **Kasteel
Tudor** (Tudor Castle; www.kasteeltudor.be), built in 1904, is
now a classy restaurant and seminar centre.

## Tillegembos

Bus No. 25 will take you to the woods of **Tillegembos** in
Bruges' southwestern suburb, Sint-Michiels. They cover an
area of 80 hectares (200 acres), providing a real rural retreat
that is a delight if you need a break from the city. Lots of
well-marked footpaths lead you around this former estate,
and there are also bridle paths, a lakeside inn, a picturesque
mill and play areas for children. Elegant, moated **Kasteel
Tillegem**, a fortress dating from the 14th century, is today
the headquarters of the West Flanders Tourist Office.

## Kasteel Loppem

**29** Situated just 3km (2 miles) south of Bruges, the **Kasteel** (Castle) at Loppem is a fine example of neo-Gothic architecture, conceived by August Pugin (architect of the British Houses of Parliament) and later completed by Jean Béthune. Built between 1858 and 1863, the structure appears from a distance to be a mass of verticals, all eaves and roof and pinnacles, accentuated by its reflection in the lake before it. Inside, the house is sumptuously decorated, the tone dominated by the wood of the ceilings and furniture. It has a private chapel and a wonderful, soaring hall.

Residences along
Ghent's Korenlei

# GHENT

**Ghent** (Gent in Dutch; Island in French), lies at the confluence of the rivers Scheldt and Leie. The city is a little larger than Bruges, but most of its historic attractions are clustered together within walking distance of one another. It is a city built on diverse economic interests, with the sense to preserve its historical heart. That past is shown in some magnificent buildings, second only to those of Bruges in splendour. Many are being renovated and there is still much to do. The inland port city has an almost Mediterranean air

**30**

about it, with the tables of cafés and bars spilling out onto the pavements.

Our tour starts from Sint-Baafsplein. Most of Ghent's historic Inner Town lies northwest of this square, straddling the Y-shaped meeting of the two rivers. This area is one of winding streets and alleyways, while the south is lined with elegant boulevards and imposing mansions.

## Sint-Baafskathedraal

The largely Gothic brick and granite **Sint-Baafskathedraal** ◄ **A**
(St Bavo's Cathedral; www.sintbaafskathedraal-gent.be; Apr–Oct Mon–Sat 8.30am–6pm, Sun 1–6pm, Nov–Mar Mon–Sat 8.30am–5pm, Sun 1–5pm; free. Mystic Lamb chapel and crypt Apr–Oct Mon–Sat 9.30am–5pm, Sun 1–5pm; Nov–Mar Mon–Sat 10.30am–4pm, Sun 1–4pm; charge) was constructed over the course of several centuries, the chancel dating from the turn of the 14th century, both the tower and the nave from the 15th century, and the transept from the mid-16th century. In the nave a forest of stone leads the eye upwards to a glorious late Gothic display

### Who Painted the Altarpiece?

Whether or not Van Eyck really was responsible for *The Adoration of the Mystic Lamb* has in the past been a matter of some dispute. An inscription on the frame of the altarpiece declares that it was started by a Hubert van Eyck and completed by his brother Jan. However, since no one has any other evidence for the existence of Hubert, it is thought by many that he was the mythical creation of Ghent citizens jealous of Bruges' monopolising of Jan. Certainly, it is difficult to believe that an artist of Van Eyck's genius could be surpassed by someone who has otherwise left nothing to posterity, and most art historians today unhesitatingly attribute the work of this painting solely to the master artist Jan van Eyck.

of rib vaulting in the roof. The tower contains a carillon, and the crypt retains some of the structure of an earlier Romanesque church.

The cathedral's greatest treasure is located in a side chapel to the left of the main entrance. Variously known as the *Ghent Altarpiece* or *The Adoration of the Mystic Lamb*, this marvellous panel painting is regarded as the crowning achievement of Jan van Eyck's Gothic style, which broke completely with medieval ideas and styles and instituted a new kind of realism.

The altarpiece seems to become increasingly detailed the closer you look at it, and the painting is invested with humanity and optimism, with God the Father looking kindly upon it all. If you look carefully, you will see Bruges Cathedral in the background of the central panel.

There are many other important works of art in the cathedral. Rubens' painting of 1624, *The Conversion of St Bavo*, is full of the unique drama with which the artist infused all his work. Also of interest is Frans Pourbus the Elder's *Christ Among the Doctors*, painted in 1571. A youthful Jesus is shown amazing the elders of the temple with his knowledge and wisdom, but it is his audience that claims our attention: Pourbus portrayed contemporary luminaries such as Philip II and Charles V, Thomas Calvin, and even his rival, painter Pieter Brueghel the Elder in the crowd. Down in the crypt is the striking *Calvary Tryptych* of Justus van Gent, painted in 1466.

## Tourist office

Ghent's tourist office is based in the crypt of the Belfort (Belfry). It is open daily Apr–Oct 9.30am–6.30pm, Nov–Mar 9.30am–4pm.

You will also find splendid examples of sculpture, the best of which is the Baroque oak and marble pulpit, one of Laurent Delvaux's masterpieces, completed in 1741. The dynamic, intricate carving of the design sweeps the eye up to where the preacher would stand, above which a marble tree of knowledge grows complete with gilded serpent and fruit. St Bavo himself is commemorated in the Baroque high altar of sculptor Hendrik Frans Verbruggen.

## The Belfort and Lakenhalle

**B** ▶ Opposite the cathedral, the **Belfort** (Belfry), completed in 1380, has since become the pre-eminent symbol of the city's independence (mid-Mar–mid-Nov daily 10am–6pm; charge). During opening times *(see above)*, a vertiginous lift ascent to the

The towering Belfry opposite the cathedral

top of the 91m (298ft) tower will reward you with spectacular views across the city.

The gilded copper dragon at the top of the spire was first installed upon completion of the tower, but the creature and the four figures now poised at the corners of the viewing platform are modern replicas. The spire itself was restored at the beginning of the 20th century according to the original 14th-century design. The impressive workings of the clock and the 52-bell carillon can be closely inspected on the fourth floor.

Together with the Belfort, the neighbouring **Lakenhalle** (Cloth Hall) magnificently expresses Ghent's civic pride and wealth. The building, much restored, dates from 1441, once serving as the meeting place for the city's wool and cloth traders. Sadly, the interior is relatively empty today.

## Botermarkt and Hoogpoort

Across the road from the Lakenhalle in Botermarkt stands the formidable **Stadhuis** (Town Hall; guided tours May–Oct Mon–Thur 3pm; charge) – all pilasters and windows. The Stadhuis is like a catalogue of architecture: the oldest part of the building (on the Hoogpoort side) dates from the early 16th century and, with its florid design and ornate statues, follows the style of Bruges' Stadhuis. Religious disputes in 1539 and the economic decline of Ghent halted the work for some 60 years. Work began again with the Renaissance-style facade of the Botermarkt side of the hall; it was continued in the 18th century with the Baroque facade facing the corner of Hoogpoort and Stadhuissteeg and the rococo Poeljemarkt side. The throne room and an impressive city council room are accessible to visitors. The guided tours are well worth joining.

North from St Baafsplein, Hoogpoort runs northwest past some beautiful Ghent houses. On the corner with the square stands **Sint-Jorishof**, the former house of the Guild of Crossbowmen (now a hotel), built in 1477. It was here that Mary of Burgundy granted a charter of freedoms to the Flemish cloth towns *(see page 16)*. Hoogpoort leads to Groentenmarkt, site of the medieval pillory and former fishmarket.

### Canal cruises

Like Bruges, Ghent offers canal boat cruises in summer. It is also fun to tour the city by tram: the main tram terminus is outside Sint-Pieters train station.

The **Groot Vleeshuis**, on the west side of the square, comprises a complex of gabled buildings restored in 1912 but dating from 1406. The buildings include a covered meat market, a guild house and a chapel.

Korenmarkt (Corn Market) connects via Kortemunt with Groentenmarkt; at its southern end stands the landmark **Sint-Niklaaskerk** (St Nicholas' Church), from where Sint- ◀ **D** Michielsbrug (St Michael's Bridge) spans the Leie River. The oldest parts of the Gothic Sint-Niklaaskerk date back to the 13th century, but the building was not completed until five centuries later. Inside, the Baroque high altar is a typically energetic design of the period. The whole church is flooded with a beautiful light on sunny days. This area offers some of the most characteristic views of Ghent; you can make out the towers of the Belfry and Sint-Baaf's Cathedral, the picturesque Korenlei and Graslei quaysides, and the ominous mass of Gravensteen, the Castle of the Counts. Across from the bridge you will see **Sint-Michielskerk** (St Michael's Church), which acts as a kind of visual counterbalance to Sint-Niklaaskerk.

A boat tour is a fun way to see Ghent

## Korenlei and Graslei

North from Sint-Michielsbrug, you can stroll on both banks of the river, past a splendid array of medieval guild houses on the quaysides. **Korenlei**, on the left, and **Graslei**, on the right, comprise Ghent's oldest harbour, the **Tussen Bruggen** (Between the Bridges). This area was the commercial heart of the medieval city and the place where Ghent's wealthy guilds chose to build.

Along Korenlei, buildings to watch out for include the **Gildehuis van de Onvrije Schippers** (House of the Tied Boatmen), at No. 7, built in 1739, an excellent example of Flemish Baroque, with spectacular dolphins and lions adorning the gables and a gilded ship crowning the roof; and the 16th-century **De Zwane** (The Swan) at No. 9, a former brewery that has a graceful swan depicted in two carvings on the gables.

Cross the Leie River on Sint-Michielsbrug to Sint-Michielskerk

Look over the water to Graslei for a view of the even finer houses on that quay before crossing for a closer inspection. The **Gilde-huis van de Vrije Schippers** (House of the Free Boatmen) was built in 1531, in Bra-

**Van Dyck**

Sint-Michielskerk contains a melancholy *Crucifixion* (1629) by Anton van Dyck, who was more famous for his portraits than his religious works.

bant Gothic style, while next door, the second Baroque **Gildehuis van de Graanmeters** (House of the Grain Weighers) dates back to 1698.

The little **Tolhuisje** (Customs House), built in 1682 in a narrow alley, looks like an attractive Renaissance after-thought. Next door is the Romanesque-style **Het Spijker**, also known as Koornstapelhuis (a former grain warehouse), dating from about 1200, and on the other side is the Koren-metershuis (Corn Measurer's house), followed by the Gothic **Gildehuis van de Metselaars** (House of the Masons), dat-ing from 1527 and built in Brabant Gothic style.

## North of Korenlei

Jan Breydelstraat branches off from the north end of Koren-lei. At No. 5, occupying a house built in 1755 by the De Con-inck family, is the **Design Museum Gent** (Tue–Sun 10am–6pm; charge). It is devoted to interior design and fur-nishings in rooms decorated mainly in 18th-century style. There is also a wonderful Art Nouveau collection, the best in the country, and some fine examples of Art Deco, as well as more modern pieces.

Further along, in adjacent Burgstraat, the Renaissance-gabled house decorated with portraits of the Counts of Flan-ders is the **Huis der Gekroonde Hoofden** (House of the Crowned Heads), now housing a restaurant of the same name tel: 09-233 37 74.

## Gravensteen

Turning right onto St Veerleplein leads to the heavily renovated island fortress called the **Gravensteen** (Castle of the
Counts; daily Apr–Sept 9am–6pm, Oct–Mar 9am–5pm;
charge). The castle is still a powerful and ominous presence
here, with massive fortifications comprising crenelled cylin-
drical towers and a vast brooding keep.

Work began on the structure in 1180 on the orders of Philip
of Alsace, on the site of a 9th-century castle. The building was
closely modelled on the Crusader castles of the Holy Land; a
climb along the battlements (particularly at the top of the keep)
provides excellent views and a welcome blast of fresh air. A
tunnel leads to the central courtyard, which is surrounded by
turreted walls, and the central keep may be reached via a
spiral staircase. Inside, the keep contains the living quarters of
a succession of Counts of Flanders, including the impressive

**The forbidding bulk of the Gravensteen**

Great Hall where Philip the Good fêted the Knights of the Golden Fleece in 1445.

## From Kraanlei to Vrijdagmarkt

Kraanlei is lined with fine houses; at No. 65 the almshouses are now home to **Het Huis van Alijn** (Alijn House; huisvanalijn.be; Tue–Sun 11am–5pm; charge), the city's folklore museum. Built in 1363, this beautifully restored complex is comprised of 18 interconnected cottages arranged around a courtyard. Each room is decorated in the style typical of the years around 1900. The everyday life of working people is evoked through the items and tools they would have known and used and the few luxuries they could afford.

Crossing the Leie via the Zuivelbrug leads to Grootkannonplein, where you will meet **Dulle Griet** (Mad Meg) – a 16-ton cannon made in the 15th century, standing on the quayside, supported by three stone plinths.

Just a few steps away, **Vrijdagmarkt** (Friday Market) has some excellent examples of guild houses, with a 19th-century monument to Ghent hero Jacob van Artevelde at the centre of the square. The stylish Art Nouveau building named **Ons Huis**, which was built in 1900, used to belong to the Socialist Workers' Association; it is attractive in itself, though it appears too tall for the square. Older houses include Nos 22 and 43–7, built in the 17th and 18th centuries respectively.

In this square the Flemish Counts were sworn in by the citizens of the city. Visible from the square in Koningstraat, the **Koninklijke Vlaamse Academie** (Royal Flemish Academy) is an imposing Baroque mansion that looms over the entire length of the street.

## Around Veldstraat

Veldstraat, running south from Sint-Niklaaskerk, is the city's main shopping street, as you will soon realise from the crowds (the street is pedestrianised, but watch out for trams). Many of the original building exteriors remain. The most historic and flamboyant of these is the **Hote d'Hane-Steenhuyse**. The eye-catching rococo facade of this 18th-century mansion is matched only by the classical facade of its garden frontage. Louis XVIII lived here briefly when he fled from Napoleon; other inhabitants have included the French writer and statesman Talleyrand and members of the Russian royal family.

At No. 82, the **Museum Arnold Vander Haeghen** (Mon–Fri 8am–noon, 2–5pm; free) is devoted to the library of Nobel Prize-winning writer Maurice Maeterlinck (1862–1949) and Ghent graphic artist Victor Stuyvaert. The house was built in 1741; in 1815 it was home to the Duke of Wellington. It has a charming Chinese salon with silk wallpaper and some 18th- and 19th-century interior designs; it also hosts a variety of temporary exhibitions.

Turn left at Zonnestraat to **Kouter** and you will find yourself in a large square that has good claim to being the most historically significant one in the city. A variety of festivals, military parades, political demonstrations, meetings, archery contests and tournaments have taken place here through the centuries, and a flower market has been held in the square on Sunday since the 18th century. It may be difficult to envisage all the pomp of the past, as very few buildings of any antiquity have survived; exceptions to this are the house at No. 29 and the Opera House, situated off the square in Schouwburgstraat, and completed in 1840.

Sint-Niklaaskerk, the Belfort and Sint-Baafskathedraal

A riot of colour at the Sunday flower market at Kouter

## Fine Arts Museum

A 10-minute walk along Charles de Kerchovelaan leads to **Citadelpark**. In the eastern corner of the park is the **Museum voor Schone Kunsten** (Museum of Fine Arts; www.mskgent.be; Tue–Sun 10am–6pm; charge). The strange art of Hieronymus Bosch is represented by *Christ Carrying the Cross*, an unforgettable painting showing Christ on the way to Calvary. The artist emphasises the characters accompanying Jesus – a procession of grotesques.

Among other Flemish and Dutch exhibits are works by Jacob Jordaens, Frans Hals' bravura *Old Lady* – full of exuberant brushwork – Pieter Brueghel the Younger's *Peasant Wedding* and a rather harassed *Village Advocate*. Rubens is represented by a *Scourging of Christ* and *St Francis Receiving the Stigmata*. Later paintings include works by Géricault, Corot, Courbet, Daumier, Ensor and Rouault. The former casino opposite the Museum of Fine Arts is now occupied by **Stedelijk Museum voor Actuele Kunst**, **SMAK** (Museum of Contemporary Art; www.smak.be; Tue–Sun 10am–6pm; charge). The permanent collection is mainly devoted to Belgian and international artists since 1945, with works by Bacon, Panamarenko, Broodthaers, Long and Nauman. The museum also has a reputation for outstanding temporary exhibitions.

## Sint-Pietersplein

North of the museum, Overpoortstraat leads to Sint-Pieter-splein, where there are regular exhibitions of art and other cultural events at the **Kunsthal Sint-Pietersabdij** (St Peter's Abbey Arts Centre; Tue–Sun 10am–6pm; charge).

The Baroque dome
of Sint-Pieterskerk

The splendid 57m (188ft) cupola of **Onze-Lieve-Vrouw Sint-Pieterskerk** (Church of Our Lady of St Peter) can be seen for many streets around. The Baroque church was designed by the Huyssens brothers and built in 1719. Clearly, the architects were not lacking in ambition: the design is based on St Peter's Basilica in Rome. The impressive façade dominates attractive Sint-Pietersplein; the church has an exuberant Baroque-style interior and artworks by Van Dyck. From Sint-Pietersplein, Sint-Kwintens-berg leads to Nederkouter, and then Veldstraat.

## How Flanders Influenced Art

Medieval Flanders bequeathed some of the most profound and best-loved paintings to the world, the greatest of which can be seen in Bruges and Ghent. The brilliance of painters such as Bosch, Memling and Van Eyck sprang from the Gothic tradition that nurtured them. Gothic art was essentially a religious artform, with devotional paintings depicting the life of Christ, the Virgin Mary and the saints, but in Flanders it also came to place great emphasis on the accurate representation of the world, which was seen as God's creation and a vehicle for the sacred.

Van Eyck retained the religious subject matter of the Gothic tradition, but used the revolutionary medium of oil, enabling him to paint with greater control. No artist before him had observed nature so minutely, or was capable of rendering observations so precisely. His paintings (including his *Madonna with Canon George Van der Paele*, in Bruges, and the famous *Ghent Altarpiece*, in Sint-Baafskathedraal), along with those of Memling and artists such as Petrus Christus, Hugo van der Goes and Pieter Pourbus, reinforce this truthfulness to appearance.

The combination of sacred theme and faithful depiction of the world was taken a stage further a hundred years after Van Eyck in the work of Brueghel the Elder, whose paintings of biblical events are set in the recognisable peasant world of his time.

Nevertheless, the genius of an artist usually needs fertile soil in which to grow. For a long time the wealth of the Burgundian court and the merchant class of Bruges and Ghent was enough to pay for the commissioning of new works.

Eventually, however, the economic centre of gravity moved northward to Antwerp (home to Rubens and his pupil Van Dyck) and the Netherlands, where the first sophisticated market for genre paintings developed. Inevitably, the influence of Flemish painting moved with the money. Yet its preoccupations were to filter through the artistic world for centuries to come.

# WHAT TO DO

## SHOPPING

The thought of shopping in Bruges may not immediately leap to mind, but the city has a large range of stores of all descriptions. Bruges is adapted to the lucrative tourist trade so you will find plenty of specialised stores and souvenirs. Except for certain items, such as beer bought at the supermarket, and chocolates, prices are probably what you would expect to pay at home.

### Where to Shop

The main shopping street is Steenstraat, off the Markt, which has everything you would expect in the way of shops catering to everyday local needs, including clothes, shoes, food, home furnishings and electrical goods. There are also a few shops that sell Belgian chocolates and other souvenirs. The street and its associated malls become very crowded on Saturday, when the best time to go is first thing in the morning.

Bruges' network of small city-centre streets and alleys conceals a surprising number of shops, most of them specialising in items such as lace, chocolate or clothes. Particular streets to look around are those surrounding the Burg and the Markt.

Take a ride around the city in a horse-drawn carriage

### Shopping hours

Shopping hours are from 9 or 9.30am to 5.30 or 6pm; many smaller shops close for an hour at lunch time. Late-night shopping tends to be on Friday, with many stores open until 7 or 7.30pm. Shops that cater mainly to tourists (which in Bruges is just about all of them) usually open on Sunday.

### Tax-free?

Tax-free shopping is available in stores that display the appropriate notice – usually the larger or more expensive specialised stores. If you're not sure, ask for details in the shop itself (see also page 128).

Most of the city's squares have few shops: the Markt and the Burg are bounded by historical buildings with some cafés and restaurants; Jan van Eyckplein has none; and 't Zand is all bistros and hotels. An exception is Sint-Jansplein.

Bruges has a number of markets. The main one is on Wednesday on the Markt, and there is a bric-a-brac and craft market on 't Zand and Beursplein on Saturday (both open 7am–1pm). Don't miss the excellent antiques and flea market that takes place along the Dijver canal from March to October on Saturday and Sunday from noon–5pm. A huge flea market is held three times a year (in July, August and September) in Koning Albertpark and 't Zand Square.

## Good Buys

**Antiques.** These are plentiful and are sold mostly in small, intimidatingly expensive-looking stores in the narrow side streets off the main shopping areas. A good example is Antiek Fimmer-Van der Cruysse, Sint-Salvatorskerkhof 18 (tel: 050-34 20 25), which deals in mahogany furniture, silver work and glassware.

**Beer.** This is an essential purchase for connoisseurs, with many brands on sale that are simply not available elsewhere. You will need a car to carry significant quantities. The range of Belgian beers is vast, so it's safest to stick to those you have tried and liked rather than risk being disappointed by an unknown. Note that it is much cheaper to buy beer at conventional supermarkets, but they may not stock your favourites. A good place to try in Bruges is the delicatessen Deldycke at

Wollestraat 23 (tel: 050-33 43 35; www.deldycke.be), which stocks Bruges beers and 12-bottle selection crates.

**Chocolate.** 'Made in Belgium', probably the best in the world, is available everywhere. It is best to avoid the tourist-oriented products, such as the chocolate rabbits, and concentrate on the incomparable delights of the classic, exquisite, handmade Belgian praline and truffle. Selection boxes (either pre-packed, or filled with your own choices) can be bought in a range of weights and are always gift-wrapped attractively. Prices vary hugely, with items stocked in hotel foyers the worst value for money.

A good shop in Bruges is Chocolatier Van Oost at Wolle-straat 11 (tel: 050-33 14 54; www.chocolatiervanoost.be), a small store with a select range. Other fine outlets worth visiting are Pralinette, at Wollestraat 31B (tel: 050-34 83

Exquisite handmade chocolates are everywhere
– and hard to resist

83; www.pralinette.be), and Verheecke, at Steenstraat 30 (tel: 050-33 22 86).

**Food and wine.** Purchases may be limited by your tastes and appetites, the time of year, the freshness of the produce, or even the size of your car, but it would be a shame not to come away with something, even if it is just for your return journey. Belgium is justly celebrated for its pâtisseries and cakes, and there are some superb specialist food shops and delicatessens in Bruges. Pâtisserie Prestige at Vlamingstraat 12 (tel: 050-34 31 67) has an equally delectable selection, while the aforementioned Delicatessen Deldycke at Wollestraat 23 has an excellent range of fine foods and wines.

**Lace.** Lace was once the principal product made in Bruges and is certainly the premier souvenir today. In the course of your strolls through the city you are likely to see enough lace shops to satisfy even the most ardent admirer of this delicate

Bruges is a great place to buy quality foodstuffs

fabric. Although most lace on sale is machine-made, usually in the Far East, handmade lace in the distinctive *duchesse* (duchess), *bloemenwerk* (flower lace), *rozenkant* (pearled rosary), and *toveressesteek* (fairy stitch) styles can still be found. Some shops deal exclusively in the handmade product, which has a Quality Control label and is, of course, more expensive, but most shops sell a mix of the two. Breidelstraat (connecting the Markt with the Burg)

Handmade Belgian lace is easy to find – but expensive

is the city's lace alley, but it is sold throughout the city, so you will have plenty of choice. Reliable sources of guaranteed, authentic Belgian handmade lace are the family-run Lace Jewel, at Philipstockstraat 11 (tel: 050-33 42 25), Melissa, Katelijnestraat 38 (tel: 050-33 45 32) and Selection, Breidelstraat 10–12 (tel: 050-33 11 86).

## ENTERTAINMENT

Walking, watching, eating and drinking are the chief pleasures of Bruges, but you can tour the city by boat and by horse-drawn carriage – peaceful and relaxing ways to see the sights *(see page 123)*.

Bruges café society mainly takes place indoors, since space and city preservation rules allow little else (although tables do appear outside in the summer, and some pedestrianised squares, like handsome little Huidenvettersplein, provide exceptions to this rule).

Bicycles are easy to rent *(see page 112)* and the city is flat, though you will have to cope with the cobblestones. From Bruges, you can easily cycle to Damme *(see page 57)* along the canal.

## Nightlife

**Music, opera, theatre.** There are regular music festivals and concerts throughout the year, and the city tourist office will have the latest information. Bruges has performances of classical music, opera and dance at the Concertgebouw, in 't Zand Square, and at the Stadsschouwburg, Vlamingstraat 29. Hotels and churches frequently host a variety of concerts and recitals.

**Cinemas.** International films are usually shown in their original language, with subtitles. The tourist office in Bruges can tell you what's on; the main cinema is Lumière in Sint-Jacobsstraat (tel: 050-34 34 65; www.lumiere.be), while Liberty in Kuipersstraat (tel: 050-33 20 11) has the occasional off-beat film.

**Nightclubs.** In Ghent, most clubs are to be found in the Zuid Quarter, but Bruges has little to offer those who want to dance the night away. It tends to be quiet at night. The Cactus Club@MaZ, Magdalenastraat 27 (tel: 050-33 20 14; www.cactusmusic.be), in the suburb of Sint-Andries, is one of Bruges' most adventurous venues, with its electro-industrial and frontline-assembly bands, as well as nostalgia events like rock-and-roll dances.

The lounge-bar at the chic brasserie-restaurant B-IN, in the Oud Sint-Jan complex between Mariastraat and Zonnekemeers (tel: 050-31 13 00; www.b-in.be), has

**Events guide**

Bruges Tourist Office issues a free publication, *events@brugge*, which lists entertainment and events in the city.

regular DJ evenings. Equally hip kaffee L'aMaRaL, Kuipersstraat 10 (tel: 0497-39 19 29; www.lamaral.be) serves up cocktails and has both local and international DJs. The multipurpose venue De Werf, at Werfstraat 108 (tel: 050-330529, www.dewerf.be) in the northern harbour district, is best known for good jazz and theatrical performances (in Dutch) , and also puts on a number of events for children.

**Bars.** 't Brugs Beertje, Kemelstraat 5 (tel: 050-33 96 16; www.brugsbeertje.be), a popular traditional café, has more than 300 ales on its menu. Old World atmosphere is built into the city's oldest tavern, Café Vlissinghe, Blekersstraat 2 (tel: 050-34 37 37; www.cafevlissinghe.be), which dates from 1515. If you are a fan of both Spanish tapas and the Blues, you will find this somewhat unlikely combo at Vino Vino, Grauwwerkersstraat 15 (tel: 050-34 51 15). At De Versteende Nacht, Langestraat 11 (tel: 050-34 32 93), you can have a

Bruges by night is delightful, but nightlife is fairly quiet

meal and a drink, read strip-cartoon books (or look at them – they're in Dutch) and listen to jazz from Bebop to modern. The music café Ma Rica Rokk, 't Zand 7–8 (tel: 050-33 83 58; www.maricarokk.be) is noisy enough to appeal to youthful spirits who can handle techno while they drink; while Boru at Burg 8 (tel: 050-34 45 02) is an Irish bar-cum-restaurant that has regular evenings of Irish music.

## SPORTS

Switch on any hotel television and you will soon learn that football (soccer) is the top spectator sport. Bruges has its own football team, Club Brugge KV (www.club brugge.be), which is often a challenger for national and European honours, and plays its home games at the Jan Breydelstadion in the Sint-Andries district, to the west of the historic centre of the city. It shares the stadium with the enthusiastic but far less successful local side Cercle Brugge (www.cerclebrugge.be).

Cycling and skating are also popular activities here, and

**Getting friendly with a dolphin at Boudewijn Seapark**

when you are in Bruges, you can obtain information about all aspects of sport and recreation from Sportdienst Brugge (tel: 050-72 70 00). Many sports facilities are in the suburbs, but are easily reached from the city centre. In Bruges, there are swimming pools in Sint-Kruis and Sint-Andries; in Ghent, the Centre Blaarmeersen offers swimming, squash, tennis and athletics.

## ACTIVITIES FOR CHILDREN

**Amusement parks.** Boudewijn Seapark at A. De Baeckestraat 12 (tel: 050-38 38 38; www.boudewijnseapark.be), includes a dolphinarium with daily shows throughout the year, fairground rides, and Bobo's Indoor, a play area. De Toverplaneet at Legeweg 88 (tel: 0478-22 69 29; www.detoverplaneet.be), is an indoor playground that is open Wednesday to Sunday and public holidays. In Zeebrugge, a harbour-side theme park called **Seafront Zeebrugge** operates from June to September and is usually a winner (www.seafront.be).

By the lake in Ghent's Citadelpark

**Museums and attractions.** Most museums in Bruges will only appeal to older children, but there are some exceptions. And if they have heads for heights, children should love climbing the Belfry.

**Puppet theatre.** In the second half of July at the Ghent Festival you can see traditional puppet theatre, which is bound to enthuse younger children.

**Tours.** Canal boat tours and horse-drawn carriage rides are both popular with children *(see page 123)*, and you can rent bicycles of sizes to suit the whole family and explore at the children's pace *(see page 112)*.

# Calendar of Events

For the most up-to-date information (specific dates, etc) on the festivals and arts calendar in Bruges, consult the tourist office. The following list gives an idea of some of the major events taking place throughout the year.

**March** *Bruges:* Cinema Novo Film Festival, held at various venues across the city.

**May** *Bruges:* Ascension Day Procession of the Holy Blood – an historical and ecclesiastical pageant. The *Dwars door Brugge* road race is also held in Bruges in May. *Ypres:* Kattenstoet (Festival of the Cats) – a colourful medieval pageant that features cats (velvet cats!) being thrown from the Belfry by the town jester; takes place every three years (next due in 2012).

**July–August** *Bruges:* Zandfeesten, the largest flea market in Flanders (held on Sundays).

**July** *Bruges:* Festival of Flanders – a major festival of classical music that takes place over months throughout Flanders; venues in Bruges include concert halls, churches and historic buildings. *Ghent:* Ghent Festival – a range of musical and cultural festivities take place in the city centre in a massive 10-day street festival.

*Bruges:* Cactus Festival – celebrating world music at Minnewater.

**August** *Bruges:* Festival of the Canals – a nocturnal pageant along the illuminated canals that takes place every three years (next due in 2011). Early Music Festival, various venues. Pageant of the Golden Tree – commemoration once every five years of the wedding of Charles the Bold and Margaret of York (next due in 2012).

*Ghent:* Patersholfeesten – various festivities in the Patershol area of the city. International Chamber Music Festival at various venues.

*Zeebrugge:* Sand Sculpture Festival – stunning transformation of part of the Zeebrugge seashore into towering works of art.

**October** *Ghent:* International Film Festival.

**November** *Bruges:* International Antiques Fair.

**December** *Bruges:* Kerstmarkten, Christmas market and ice-rink at Markt and Christmas market at Simon Stevinplein. Ice sculpture festival outside the railway station. *Ghent:* Christmas market at Sint-Baafsplein.

# EATING OUT

Belgians take their eating very seriously. Their cuisine is known around the world, and most of it is of excellent quality. Portions are generous; even if you ask for a sandwich, your plate will generally arrive loaded with much more than just garnish. Regional cuisines are strongly defined, but in the cities you should have no trouble sampling dishes from all over Belgium (and beyond).

## Restaurants and Bars

Bruges and Ghent have a great many restaurants, cafés and bars from which to choose. 'Restaurant' can mean anything from a formal, top-class establishment to a small café. Bars usually serve simple, hearty food at reasonable prices. Even in the smallest place you will be served at your table so, if in doubt, simply take your seat: most waiters are pleased to speak English.

Menus are often printed in a variety of languages, and at lunch *(middagmaal)* and dinner *(avondeten)* there is often a tourist menu and a choice of set menus at fixed prices; these are the best value. Some set meals are served only at lunch time or only on particular days. Bars and cafés usually serve snacks in the morning, then lunch from around noon – times and menus are posted in the windows. Many bars stay open until the early hours.

Mussels, French fries and beer are a favourite meal

## Breakfast

Hotels serve substantial buffet breakfasts (*ontbijt*) which can see you through until lunch time with no trouble at all. Along with tea or coffee and fruit juice, there will be a variety of breads, cheeses and cold meats, plus fresh fruit and cereal, yogurt and fruit salads, buns and pastries. You may be asked if you would like a boiled egg, and some of the larger hotels also provide buffet grills, so you can have a fried breakfast as well. Even in the smaller hotels the choice on offer is usually large and the food fresh.

## Cold Dishes

A *boterham* is an open sandwich, which you will find served just about everywhere. Usually comprising two or three huge slices of bread with the filling of your choice plus a salad, they are excellent when accompanied by a Belgian beer – and offer great value. There is an enormous range, from salmon to meat to cheeses.

## Fish and Shellfish

The close proximity of the North Sea and the traditional culture built around canal and river mean that fish dominates most menus. Alas, the canals of Bruges and Ghent are now virtually lifeless, but freshwater fish are brought to the table from further afield.

One great favourite is fresh mussels (*mosselen*) in season (from Zeeland, in Holland), which are advertised everywhere when they are available, generally between mid-July and mid-February. Served simply

### Extras

Value-added tax (BTW) is nearly always included in the bill (so is a service charge, although this is not always the case), so there is usually no need to tip unless you want to. But it is customary to leave at least the small change.

Dining out in Bruges offers something for every taste

with wedges of lemon, or cooked in a cream, white wine, or garlic and parsley sauce, they are a great delicacy and frequently arrive in a large pan from which diners help themselves. Mussels are best eaten with that other great Belgian staple, *frieten* (French fries).

Trout *(forel)* is another firm favourite, often served in a sauce of white wine, and eel *(aal or paling)* crops up on menus a lot, frequently in thick sauces with herbs: *paling in 't groen* ('green eel') is boiled eel with green herbs. Fresh sole *(zeetong)* is mostly served grilled, while oysters, lobsters and crab are dressed in a variety of sauces. Many restaurants have a tank of lobsters or crabs on view to entice customers and prove the freshness of the dish.

The local coast delivers other types of seafood, such as herring, mostly from Nieuwpoort, which may be lightly salted on the boat and eaten raw as *maatjes*. Herring are also popular – and delicious – when served smoked, steamed,

marinated, or in a rich, red wine sauce *(bonne femme)*.

Fish can also feature in the traditional *waterzooi*, a delicately flavoured stew made with vegetables and fish (or sometimes chicken). *Waterzooi op Gentse wijze*, a dish orginating from Ghent, is always made with fish.

## Meat and Poultry

Game, pork and beef play a prominent part in the Flemish diet, alongside a variety of chicken dishes. *Carbonnade* is a classic Belgian dish of beef casseroled in beer, with onions and herbs. There are steaks of fine quality, too, usually served with *frieten* (French fries).

Succulent steaks are bound to please carnivores

You may also come across goose *(gans)*, first boiled and then roasted. Veal *(kalf)* and liver *(lever)* dishes are also widely available. During the game season, rabbit or hare cooked in Gueuze beer with onions and prunes *(konijn met pruimen)* appear on many menus, as well as rich pheasant dishes in thick sauces. *Wildzwijn* is wild boar, which comes from the Ardennes, and has lots of flavour.

## Vegetables and Salads

You will find *witloof* (chicory) on most menus, served in a ham andcheese sauce; *stoemp*, a mixture of mashed potatoes and other vegetables, is often served with sausages.

Salad *(sla, salade)* is very much an incidental on Belgian menus, where meat and fish rule supreme. Salads to look out for include the *liégoise*, which contains green beans and potatoes and is served luke-warm, and the *wallonie*, which features a combination of potatoes and bacon.

## Cheese

Cheese *(kaas)* comes in an enormous number of different types, most of them Belgian, Dutch or French. Belgium alone produces 300, including Trappist cheeses such as Orval and Chimay. Belgian Gouda and Remoudou are some of the better-known names. Meals traditionally end with cheese, so leave some room for it if it is on the menu.

## Desserts and Pâtisseries

The Belgians love a good dessert, and the more chocolate and cream it has the better. *IJs* (ice cream) and *slagroom* (whipped cream) are usually involved somewhere, perhaps oozing from pancakes or waffles. The ideal way to round off a meal of mussels and *frieten* is with a *dame blanche* – vanilla ice cream and rich, hot chocolate sauce. The selection of cakes, fruit tarts, pastries, buns and biscuits available is immense.

You will find a wide selection of tarts and pastries

## Snacks

French fries are the staple snack of both Bruges and Ghent, sold from stalls and vans dotted around the streets. They can be topped with a variety of calorie-laden sauces: ketchup, mayonnaise, mustard curry –

you name it. There are fast-food places all over the towns – in Bruges, they are found mostly around the Markt, 't Zand and Steenstraat, and in Ghent you will see them in Vrijdag-markt and the Veldstraat area.

Bars generally serve light snacks such as *Croque Monsieur* (toasted ham and cheese sandwich) and *Toast Cannibal* (toast topped with steak tartar), plus open sandwiches and filled rolls *(belegde broodje).*

## Vegetarians

Although the Belgian diet is dominated by fish and meat, it is not difficult to adhere to a varied vegetarian regime in Bruges and Ghent. However, this usually means foregoing traditional Flemish cooking. Listed in the Recommended Restaurants section *(see page 104)* are a number of places that serve vegetarian food. Be careful when ordering not to confuse vegetarian with *vleesgerecht*, which is a meat dish, and to remember also that the Belgian French fry *(friet)* is likely to have been cooked in animal fat. Some 'vegetarian' restaurants also serve meat and fish. If you cannot find a specialist eating house, head for one of the many Italian restaurants – non-meat pasta dishes and salads are usually offered as a matter of course.

## Drinks

Coffee *(koffie)* is fairly strong and usually served with extras such as little biscuits or chocolates, plus two or three kinds of sugar. Coffee liqueurs (especially Irish coffee) are popular and available everywhere. Tea *(thee)* is often served in a glass with lemon and without milk. Herbal teas are widely available.

Some of Belgium's many varieties of beer *(bier)* are de-scribed on *page 102*. Most bars stock at least 20 or 30, and a few will have more than 100. Those on tap *(van 't vat)* are cheaper than the bottled kind. All the usual spirits are available in generous measures. *Jenever* is the indigenous gin, and it is very strong. Most of the wine *(wijn)* is imported from France and Germany.

Essential bars to visit in Bruges are: 't Brugs Beertje at Kemelstraat 5, where the friendly and knowledgeable landlord will advise you on all aspects of his 300 or so beers; and De Garre, in the alley of the same name off Breidelstraat, which has a comfortable atmosphere and an impressive range of beers that includes its own brand. In Ghent, try Het Waterhuis aan de Bierkant, Groentenmarkt 9, a popular canalside bar with more than 100 beers on offer; De Witte Leeuw, Graslei 6, a friendly bar with more than 100 beers; and De Dulle Griet, Vrijdagmarkt 50, which has more than 250 types of beer, plus 1½-litre (2½-pint) Kwak glasses *(see next page)* on proud display.

Just a few of Belgium's hundreds of different – and excellent – beers

## Belgian Beers

Beer is to the Belgians what wine is to the French and, indeed, many Belgian beers complete the last stage of their fermentation in corked bottles. Several hundred different sorts are produced, all of which have their distinctive character – and are served in their own type of glass.

*Lambic* beers are wild beers, so called because their fermentation involves exposure to wild yeast. Many have a sour, apple-like taste, but these may have added fruit to impart the distinctive flavour. *Kriek*, a delicious cherry beer, comes in a round glass (served hot if you wish to warm up), while *Frambozen* beer is a pale pink raspberry brew served in a tall stemmed glass. White beers like the popular Hoegaarden are cloudy and generally light and youthful in flavour.

The label *Trappist* refers to a large number of beers originally brewed in monasteries. *Tripel* denotes a very strong beer that was served to the abbot and other important personages; the monks drank the *Dubbel*, while the peasants (ie everyone else) had only a watery version. *Trappist Leffe* is a strong, dark beer, like porter, slightly sweet and served in a bulbous glass.

*Kwak* (a strong, light-coloured beer) is served in a special glass with a spherical base that sits in a wooden stand in order to remain upright. The 1½-litre (2½-pint) glasses and stands are so valuable that customers must often give up a shoe to ensure they don't run off with them.

One of the strongest beers is the appropriately named *Delirium Tremens*, which can take you by surprise if you're not used to it – though if you see pink elephants, they are on the label and not in your head. Another powerful but delicious beer is *Corsendonck Agnus Dei*.

*Gueuze* is a very quaffable, honey-coloured, sweet beer served in a straight glass; *Loburg*, a Brussels-brewed light-coloured beer served in something like a vase; *Hoegaarden Grand Cru*, a refreshing, coriander-based beer; *Rodenbach Grand Cru*, a red beer with a sharp apple taste; and *Bourgogne des Flandres*, a light, flavourful red beer.

## TO HELP YOU ORDER

I'd like a/an/some …          **Heeft u …**

| | | | |
|---|---|---|---|
| **beer** | bier | **potatoes** | aardappelen |
| **bread** | brood | **salad** | sla, salade |
| **coffee** | koffie | **salt** | zout |
| **dessert** | nagerecht | **soup** | soep |
| **fish** | vis | **sugar** | suiker |
| **ice cream** | ijs | **tea** | thee |
| **meat** | vleesgerecht | **vegetables** | groenten |
| **milk** | melk | **water** | water |
| **pepper** | peper | **wine** | wijn |

## MENU READER

| | | | |
|---|---|---|---|
| **aardbei** | strawberry | **mosselen** | mussels |
| **appel** | apple | **nieren** | kidneys |
| **bonen** | beans | **oesters** | oysters |
| **boter** | butter | **peer** | pear |
| **eend** | duck | **perzik** | peach |
| **ei** | egg | **pruim** | plum |
| **garnalen** | prawns | **ree** | venison |
| **ham** | ham | **rijst** | rice |
| **haring** | herring | **rode wijn** | red wine |
| **honing** | honey | **rund** | beef |
| **kaas** | cheese | **rodekool** | red cabbage |
| **kers** | cherry | **sinaasappel** | orange |
| **kip** | chicken | **snoek** | pike |
| **koek** | cake | **taart** | flan |
| **kool** | cabbage | **varken** | pork |
| **kreeft** | lobster | **witte wijn** | white wine |
| **lam** | lamb | **worst** | sausage |
| **macaroni** | noodles | **zalm** | salmon |

# PLACES TO EAT

*Prices are for a three-course meal including tax but not drinks. The restaurants listed here accept all major credit cards unless otherwise stated.*

€€€€ above 75 euros       €€ 25–50 euros
€€€ 50–75 euros           € below 25 euros

## BRUGES

**Bhavani €€** *Simon Stevinplein 5, tel: 050-33 90 25.* Good quality and authentic Indian cuisine is served here, making this a great place if you want a change from Belgian food. Specialities are Madras and tandoori dishes; you also have vegetarian choices.

**Brasserie Erasmus €€** *In the Hotel Erasmus, Wollestraat 35, tel: 050-33 57 81.* A great place for budget dining, and all the main dishes are prepared with Belgian beer, of which the restaurant stocks 16 on tap and around 200 bottled varieties.

**Breydel–De Coninck €€** *Breidelstraat 24, tel: 050-33 97 46.* Conveniently located between the Burg and the Markt this long-standing proponent of the Belgian obsession with mussels has traditional style and wood-beamed ceilings. It serves the mollusc in a variety of ways – the most popular of which is the basic big steaming potful – and all are worth going back for. Other seafood dishes, such as lobster and eels, have a place on the menu too.

**De Belgede Boterham €** *Kleine Sint-Amandsstraat 5, tel: 050-34 91 31.* Friendly, small rustic wholefood café and pâtisserie just west of the Markt. The menu includes fresh Flemish sandwiches and salads. Open daily until 5pm.

**De Karmeliet €€€€** *Langestraat 19, tel: 050-33 82 59.* Book well in advance to eat at this triple Michelin-starred restaurant on the main street heading east from the centre of town, where chef Geert Van Hecke produces sumptuous French cuisine. Closed Sunday and Monday.

**De Koetse €€** *Oude Burg 31, tel: 050-33 76 80*. This inviting restaurant just off Simon Stevinplein has a rustic Flemish interior with a blazing fire in winter. It serves robust Flemish cooking, including spare ribs and excellent *frites*.

**De Stove €€** *Kleine Sint-Amandsstraat 4, tel: 050-33 78 35*. A small, simply decorated, intimate restaurant, just west of the Markt. Family-owned and operated, it specialises in Flemish dishes, with an emphasis on salads, fish and steaks. Closed Wednesday and Thursday.

**De Visscherie €€€€** *Vismarkt 10, tel: 050-33 02 12*. With a name like this and a location in the Vismarkt (Fish Market) it's no surprise that the speciality here is seafood, and nowhere in town does it better. An elegant interior is the setting for dishes served both nouvelle cuisine-style and in classic Belgian manner. Among the latter is a North Sea *waterzooi* (Flemish fish stew). Closed Tuesday.

**Den Dyver €€€** *Dijver 5, tel: 050-33 60 69*. This is one of the finest restaurants in Bruges, on the main canal, close to the Groeningemuseum. It turns cooking into an art-form. Closed all day Wednesday, and Thursday afternoon.

**Den Gouden Harynck €€€** *Groeninge 25, tel: 050-33 76 37*. An exceptionally fine restaurant in a brick building just west of the Groeningemuseum, that was once a fish shop (look for the sign of the herring). If there is such a thing as nouvelle Flemish cuisine, then this is where you'll find it; the wine list is superb.

**Die Swaene €€€** *Steenhouwersdijk 1, tel: 050-34 27 98*. French/Flemish cuisine is served amid elegant surroundings in the very fine hotel of the same name, just off the Vismarkt.

**Duc de Bourgogne €€€** *Huidenvettersplein 12, tel: 050-33 20 38*. For this classic Bruges dining experience, French dishes are served in baronial surroundings, with a canal view that is one of the city's most photographed.

**Het Dagelijks Brood €** *Philipstockstraat 21, tel: 050-33 60 50.* Fresh breads and cakes are on sale here, just east of the Markt, but go for breakfast, lunch or tea to revel in the family atmosphere. Sit at the enormous central table that dominates the room. Closed Tuesday. No credit cards.

**Het Mozarthuys €€** *Huidenvettersplein 1, tel: 050-33 45 30.* Guess which famous composer's music wafts among the tables at this old-style Flemish restaurant? Yes, you can hum along to Wolfgang Amadeus while you enjoy its speciality grilled meat dishes and mussels. The outdoor terrace on the pretty little square is a big draw in good weather.

**Huidevettershuis €€** *Huidenvettersplein 10, tel: 050-33 95 06.* An elegant canal-side eatery (with an entrance on a handsome little square just off Vismarkt), specialising in Flemish cuisine. The building, which was formerly the Tanners' Guild House, dates from 1630. Closed Tuesday.

**Koto €€€** *In the Hotel De Medici, Potterierei 15, tel: 050-44 31 31.* A Japanese restaurant in a four-star hotel that serves top-flight teppan yaki and classic cuisine such as sushi and tempura, accompanied by sake in typically stylish surroundings. Meat is tender and well flavoured, and vegetables have just the right degree of crunchiness. Dinner only (except Sunday lunch). Closed Monday.

**Lotus €** *Wapenmakersstraat 5, tel: 050-33 10 78.* This cool, unpreachy purveyor of vegetarian cuisine, two blocks north of the Burg, puts an emphasis on freshness and quality that should appeal to non-vegetarians as well. The choice is very limited – nearly at take it or leave it standard – with just two dishes, offered in small, medium and large portions. Very good value for the carefully prepared dishes. Lunch only. Closed Sunday.

**Maximiliaan van Oostenrijk €€** *Wijngaardplein 16–17, tel: 050-33 47 23.* Burgundian restaurant in one of the most romantic parts of the city, adjacent to the Begijnhof and the

Minnewater. Specialities include the traditional local stew, *waterzooï*, grilled meats and seafood.

**Patrick Devos €€€€** *Zilverstraat 41, tel: 050-33 55 66*. This lavishly appointed restaurant, set in a 13th-century building close to Sint-Salvatorskathedraal, serves as a showplace for chef/owner Patrick Devos' stunning creations using fresh regional produce. Closed Sunday.

**Pietje Pek €€** *Sint-Jakobsstraat 13, tel: 050-34 78 74*. Behind its notable Art Nouveau façade, this restaurant serves satisfying portions of its speciality cheese and meat fondues, as well as an eat-all-you-want menu.

**Spinola €€€** *Spinolarei 1, tel: 050-34 17 85*. Spinola is a romantic, beautifully furnished restaurant just off the picturesque Jan van Eyckplein. The food is in a class that matches the surroundings, with fish dishes a speciality. The extensive wine list features as many as 300 wines. Closed all day Sunday and Monday afternoon.

**Strijdershuis €** *In the Hotel Koffieboontje, Hallenstraat 4, tel: 050-33 80 27*. This informal café-cum-restaurant situated just off the Markt is invariably crowded. The lively clientele is usually made up mostly of young backpackers, who are attracted by the extensive set menus, which offer excellent value for money.

**'t Bourgoensche Cruyce €€€€** *Wollestraat 41–3; tel: 050-33 79 26*. This is generally regarded as one of the best, most atmospheric dining experiences in Bruges, set in a beautiful old hotel overlooking the canal, serving Flemish regional specialities. Lunch and dinner Thur–Mon.

**Tom Pouce €€** *Burg 17, tel: 050-33 03 36*. This is a large restaurant but it manages not to be impersonal, and it enjoys an unrivalled position on the Burg. Although fish and Flemish cuisine dominate the menu, the quality of the food is secondary to that of the location. Order a waffle or pancake, sit on the heated outdoor terrace and watch the world go by.

## GHENT

**Brasserie HA'** €€–€€€ *Kouter 29; tel: 09-265 91 81*. Elegant yet cool, the Handelsbeurs Theatre's café-restaurant serves refined French and Belgian cuisine – light and breezy for lunch, candle-lit romantic for dinner. A multicoloured modern chandelier graces the main dining room, and in the summer you can enjoy your meal seated on the lovely outside terrace overlooking the Ketelvaart canal. Open Mon–Sat lunch and dinner, Sun 9–11.30am.

**De Blauwe Zalm** €€€ *Vrouwebroersstraat 2; tel: 09-224 08 52*. 'The Blue Salmon', in the hip Patershol district, is renowned for inventive fish and seafood dishes. Instead of formulaic standards, its concoctions use local specialities such as asparagus, Oriental spices or Mediterranean herbs, served in a stylish modern interior or garden terrace. Closed all day Sunday and Sat and Mon lunch.

**Eethuis Avalon** € *Geldmunt 32, tel: 09-224 37 24*. Across the street from the Gravensteen fortress, Avalon offers tasty organic-vegetarian dishes such as home-made soup served with home-baked bread, and slices of savoury quiche. The antique-tiled main room is a protected monument; there is also an attractive little garden terrace.

**Jan Breydel** €€€ *Jan Breydelstraat 10, tel: 09-225 62 87*. Overlooking the tiny Appelbrug Parkje and on the banks of the canal, the Jan Breydel restaurant offers diners fine views as they enjoy their meals. Fish dominates the menu, and is often accompanied by champagne, but there are meat dishes to be had as well. Closed Monday morning and Sunday.

**Keizershof** €€ *Vrijdagmarkt 47, tel: 09-223 44 46*. On Ghent's lively market square, this large, rambling restaurant has so much space that even when it's full it won't seem crowded. Diners pile into hearty portions of Belgian and continental food, amid decor that features wooden ceiling beams, plain wood tables and fashionably tattered walls. In summer, there are outdoor tables in the courtyard.

**La Malcontenta €€** *Haringsteeg 7–9, tel: 09-224 18 01*. This Patershol-district restaurant serves one of the most specific of specialities – cuisine from the Canary Islands. This means plenty of fish, *paella*, *patatas arrugadas* (tiny new potatoes cooked in their skins in very salty water) and *mojo* sauce (made with olive oil, vinegar, garlic and coriander). Closed Sun–Tue.

**Le Grand Bleu €€€** *Snepkaai 15, tel: 09-220 50 25*. Set in a small Provençal-style house with a lovely terrace by the Leie, west of Sint-Pietersstation, this seafood specialist presents Mediterranean-influenced fish dishes and a wide range of lobster variations. A few succulent meat dishes are also on offer. Open daily for lunch and dinner.

**Pakhuis €€** *Schuurkenstraat 4, tel: 09-223 55 55*. Pakhuis is a lively brasserie south of the Sint-Niklaaskerk, offering good modern Flemish and Franco-Italian cuisine. The setting – that of an attractively restored former warehouse – is especially impressive. Oyster and seafood platters are the speciality of the house. Closed Sunday.

**Patiron €** *Sluizeken 30, tel: 09-233 45 87*. A delightful café north of the city centre, where everything is made on the premises, including some hearty soups. The main speciality, however, is quiche, with more than 80 delicious varieties to choose from. Superb vegetarian options available.

**Vier Tafels €€** *Plotersgracht 6, tel: 09-225 05 25*. Located in one of the serpentine alleys of the Patershol district, this restaurant started with just four tables, hence its name. Now considerably enlarged, it has an adventurous menu of dishes from around the world. Be warned: the spicy dishes really are spicy.

**'t Klaverblad €€€** *Corduwanierstraat 61, tel: 09-225 61 17*. While most of the neighbouring restaurants in the Patershol try to lure you with music, 'themed cuisine' and moderate prices, 't Klaverblad is unashamedly gastronomic and expensive. French food is prepared with a Flemish twist, for serious eaters who appreciate good food. Closed Tue, Wed and Sat lunch.

# A–Z TRAVEL TIPS

## A Summary of Practical Information

## A

**ACCOMMODATION** (see also CAMPING, YOUTH HOSTELS, and the list of RECOMMENDED HOTELS on page 135)

Bruges is particularly busy in the summer months, at Easter and at weekends, so it is advisable to book well in advance if you plan to visit at this time. If you are travelling in the low season or during the week, ask about discounts – many hotels do special deals from about October to March. The rates on *page 135* are averages for double rooms in high season. Service charges and taxes are included. There is often a supplement for single rooms.

There is a star rating system (indicated in the tourist information literature and by the front door of the hotel), but the number of stars bears little relation to what you may get. Some four-star hotels may have certain facilities but not be very pleasant, while hotels further down the scale can be delightful. A few hotel exteriors and foyers look splendid, but this can be deceptive. Inspect rooms first if you can.

A substantial breakfast is often included in the hotel rate, but some hotels charge extra. This can add considerably to the price, so it may be worth looking for a local café that serves a good breakfast. The Bruges tourist office also supplies a list of bed-and-breakfast accommodation in its brochure.

The tourist offices in Bruges and Ghent can provide detailed lists of hotels in each city that describe facilities, prices and contact details. They can also book rooms for you on payment of a deposit, which is then deducted from your hotel bill. If you arrive in either city without a room, try this service first.

In Bruges, contact In & Uit, 't Zand 34, 8000 Bruges, tel: 050-44 46 46, email: toerisme@brugge.be, www.brugge.be.

What's the rate per night?    **Hoeveel kost het per nacht?**

## AIRPORT (luchthaven)

Most flights into and out of Belgium use **Brussels Airport (BRU)** (tel: 0900-70-000 in Belgium; tel: +32 2-753 7753 from outside Belgium, www.brusselsairport.be) at Zaventem, 14km (9 miles) from the centre of the capital, which is served by many major airlines. It has all the facilities you would expect of an international airport.

There are train, bus and taxi connections from the airport to Brussels – the train links are the most efficient, running every 15 minutes at peak times from the airport to all three of Brussels' main stations. From these there are regular train links to Bruges; the travel time from Brussels is about an hour.

The trip by taxi from the airport to the centre of Brussels will cost you substantially more than the train, but a reduction in the taxi fare is available if you present a round-trip air ticket.

## B

## BICYCLE HIRE (RENTAL)

Bruges encourages cyclists by allowing them to travel down more than 50 one-way streets in either direction (not as dangerous as it sounds because there are special cycle lanes). The Bruges Tourist Office issues a useful guide, *5 x Bike Around Bruges*. Bikes can be hired or loaned from many sources. Some hotels put bikes at their guests' disposal – ask when you arrive. They can be hired from the railway station in Bruges and other towns by the day. A discount is offered if you present a valid train ticket. In Ghent, tandems are also available. Bikes can be left at other participating rail stations – an information leaflet is available from stations and in advance from the Belgian tourist information office. Among other hire locations in Bruges are Hotel Koffieboontje at Hallenstraat 4 (tel: 050-33 80 27) and Fietsen Popelier at Mariastraat 26 (tel: 050-34 32 62).

I'd like to hire a bicycle **Ik zou graag een fiets huren.**

## BUDGETING FOR YOUR TRIP

Bruges can be expensive, but no more so than many popular European tourist destinations, and less so in many respects than Belgium's capital, Brussels.

**Getting to Belgium.** The cost of getting to Belgium from the UK and Ireland by air varies considerably. Flying with Ryanair one way from various airports in both countries to Brussels-Charleroi Airport can cost only a few pounds or euros (plus taxes and other charges), but £20–40 (€24–€48) one way is probably nearer the average, and can easily go higher. These rates have forced carriers such as BA, BMI, Virgin Express, Aer Lingus and Brussels Airlines to cut their fares for flights into Brussels Airport.

Of the other options, going by bus from London to Bruges is likely to be the cheapest. By train, Eurostar from London St Pancras Station to Brussels offers excursion and advance-purchase tickets, as does the Channel Tunnel car-transporter. The cost of going by ferry from Britain to Zeebrugge or Ostend varies considerably depending on the route, whether travelling as a foot passenger or with a car, and whether you want a cabin. For foot passengers, the price varies from about £30 one-way on short crossings, to about £100 on long crossings.

Similarly, the cost of transatlantic flights from North America varies greatly. A ticket from a consolidator (bucket-shop), or on a special offer, might be as low as $500 return.

**Accommodation.** For a double room with bathroom and breakfast in Bruges you can pay less than €50, but for reasonable comfort and facilities, €75–100 is a more realistic starting point; a mid-range hotel will cost €100–200; and expensive hotels begin at about €200. What you get obviously varies with the location and the time of year. At the busiest times – and Bruges is very often busy – rooms can be hard to come by.

**Eating Out.** You can eat well in many Bruges restaurants for less than €20 per person for a three-course meal without wine, but a more realistic starting point would be €30–40; in mid-range establishments, expect to pay €40–60; and in expensive restaurant, more than €75.

If you are on a tight budget look for the *dagschotel* (dish of the day) or the *dagmenu* (menu of the day), available in most restaurants, which will offer a worthwhile saving. Alternatively, eat in a café (bar) that serves low-cost food – this could be a simple spaghetti bolognaise or *biefstuk met frieten/steak-friet* (steak and fries), or maybe something a little more adventurous.

**Museums.** Public museums charge €4–8 for adult admission. Privately owned attractions may cost up to €12. There are generally reduced rates for children, senior citizens and students.

**Public Transport.** A single ticket covering the city centre costs €1.20 if bought before boarding, and €2 on board the bus. A one-day pass costs €5 if bought before boarding, and €6 on board the bus; multi-day passes are available.

## C

## CAMPING

Belgium's campsites are graded from one to four stars and are usually excellently equipped. There is just one campsite in Bruges, close enough to permit easy use of public transport into the city centre: Camping Memling, Veltemweg 109, 8310 Bruges, tel: 050-35 58 45, www.vweb.be, in the Sint-Kruis district in the east of the city, though there are others farther away, and along the Belgian coast.

The Belgian tourist office will provide a camping leaflet on request. It is advisable to book pitches in advance during the high season. Spending the night in cars, caravans, mobile homes or tents by the roadside, in woods, dunes or directly on the beach is forbidden.

## CAR HIRE (*autoverhuur*; see also DRIVING and BUDGETING FOR YOUR TRIP)

With a city centre as compact as that of Bruges, a well-organised public transport bus system, and strict rules regulating parking, there is little need for a car in the city. If you want to explore the countryside around Bruges, to include the nearby coast and World War I battlefields around Ypres, you may want to hire a car for a day or two. Major car hire firms are represented in the city, and there are many local firms whose contact details you can find in the *Gouden Gids (Yellow Pages)*. If time permits you should compare prices.

The minimum age may be 20 or 25, depending on the company and the vehicle. Credit cards are almost always required for payment, and you will need to show your driving licence and passport.

Many hotels have arrangements with car hire companies that make it simple to arrange for a car, but a small extra charge will normally be made for delivery to your hotel.

**Avis**, Koningin Astridlaan 97–7, tel: 050-39 44 00, www.avis.be.
**Europcar**, Sint-Pieterskaai 48, tel: 050-31 45 44, www.europcar.be.
**Hertz**, Pathoekeweg 25, tel: 050-37 42 34, www.hertz.be.

## CLIMATE

Belgium has a temperate climate much influenced by its proximity to the sea, although obviously this influence diminishes inland. The warmest and driest weather is between April and October, but it can rain at any time of the year. Approximate monthly temperatures in Bruges are shown below.

You can obtain a current weather forecast (in French) by telephoning 0900-27 003, or going to www.meteo.be.

|  | J | F | M | A | M | J | J | A | S | O | N | D |
|---|---|---|---|---|---|---|---|---|---|---|---|---|
| °C | 5 | 6 | 10 | 13 | 19 | 21 | 23 | 22 | 20 | 14 | 8 | 6 |
| °F | 41 | 43 | 50 | 55 | 66 | 70 | 74 | 72 | 68 | 57 | 46 | 41 |

## CLOTHING

The unpredictable climate means you should be prepared for rain at any time of the year. A raincoat is advisable, but many hotels provide complimentary umbrellas. In March and April, the weather can be bright and reasonably warm, but with sudden blasts of cold wind as you turn a corner – so a light coat that can be slipped on and off is a good idea. In winter, heavy coats and sweaters are advisable. Bruges is a walking city, so take comfortable, reliable shoes that you know will not hurt your feet, and take care on the cobblestones.

Dress is generally smart but relaxed and informal, although expensive restaurants will expect male guests to wear ties.

## CRIME AND SAFETY (See also POLICE)

Its compactness and the numbers of tourists wandering its streets make Bruges extremely safe: you are seldom alone or far from the centre. There is very little crime, though obviously it makes sense to take elementary precautions with cameras, bags and personal effects. Valuables should be left in your hotel safe.

Ghent is very safe, too, but it is wise to stay clear of the small red-light district between Keizer Karelstraat and Vlaanderenstraat, and the area around Sint-Pietersstation late at night.

If you are planning on venturing far into outlying areas of either city late at night, your hotel receptionist should be able to advise you on any areas best avoided.

# D

## DISABLED TRAVELLERS

Facilities and accessibility to transport and buildings in both cities are distinctly patchy. The cobblestone streets and medieval buildings of Bruges mean access to places of interest can be challenging, particularly as ramps and railings are invariably absent. Some hotels have ramps, but planning rules for older hotels forbid the installation of lifts (elevators), so some or all of the rooms can only be reached by the staircase. Museums are often similarly restricted, and may involve numerous stairs.

Some of the larger (chain) hotels have specially designed rooms for guests with disabilities (see Recommended Hotels on page 135). There are, at most, usually two or three such rooms per hotel.

None of the public transport is equipped with lifts or ramps, and train carriages are frequently so high off the ground that one could do with a rope ladder, but assistance is available at railway stations.

At some major road crossings in both cities, textured soft paving has been installed. All travellers should be careful near the canals, which often are not railed off from the footpath or road.

Tourist information offices should be able to provide literature on the facilities that are available; Bruges tourist information office produces a map showing free parking facilities for drivers with disabilities. In the UK, information may be obtained from Holiday Care, tel: 0845-124 9971, www.holidaycare.org.uk, or from RADAR, Unit 12, City Forum, 250 City Road, London EC1V 8AF, tel: 020-7250 3222, www.radar.org.uk.

In the US, contact the Society for the Advancement of Travel for the Handicapped (SATH), 347 Fifth Avenue, Suite 610, New York, NY 10016, tel: 212-447 7284, www.sath.org.

## DRIVING (see also CAR HIRE)

To take your car into Belgium, you will need:
• an international driving licence or your own national licence (held for at least a year).
• car registration papers.
• Green Card (this does not provide cover, but is internationally recognised proof that you have insurance – not obligatory for EU countries).
• a fire extinguisher and red warning triangle and reflective jacket in case of breakdown.
• a national identity sticker for your car.
• headlight adaptors for right-hand-drive vehicles, to prevent the lights dazzling oncoming drivers.

### Driving conditions

Drive on the right, pass on the left. Though you may wish to drive to and from Bruges, it is unnecessary and ill-advised to drive within the city itself. Bruges has a complex one-way system, with narrow winding roads that in high season are clogged with pedestrians, bicycles and horse-drawn carriages. Driving in Ghent is more aggressive than in Bruges and is made more complicated by the presence of trams, which you are not allowed to overtake and to which you must give way.

Belgium's motorway system is excellent, but it and the city ringroads (like that in Bruges) can get clogged at rush hour. Other main roads in Flanders are generally very straight and free of traffic. You should note, however, that Belgium's accident record is one of the worst in Europe.

### Rules of the road

Seat belts must be worn by both driver and passengers and there are stiff penalties for speeding and drink driving. Some offences require payment of fines on the spot.

An important rule to remember is that drivers should normally yield to traffic approaching from the right. A yellow diamond-shaped sign with a white border indicates that drivers on main roads have the right of way. When the sign reappears with a diagonal line through it, then drivers must yield to traffic from the right.

### Speed limits

On motorways, the limit is 120km/h (75mph) and on other main roads it is 90km/h (55mph). In residential areas the speed limit drops to 50km/h (30mph) or even 30km/h (18mph). In all cases, lower limits may be indicated.

### Parking

There is limited parking in the city centres. Larger car and coach parks exist around the perimeter of Bruges and on the edge of Ghent's pedestrian zone; it is safer (and quicker) to use them and walk into the centre. Both tourist offices provide maps indicating car parks.

## Breakdown

Belgium's two main motoring organisations are the Touring Club de Belgique and the Royal Automobile Club de Belgique. They have reciprocal arrangements with other national motoring organisations. Motorways have emergency phones positioned at regular intervals. In case of breakdown, call Wegenhulp/Touring Secours, tel: 070-34 47 77.

## Fuel and oil

Service stations are plentiful, and most international brands of un-leaded *(loodvrij)* petrol (gasoline) and diesel are on sale.

## Road signs

International pictographs are widely used, but here are some written signs you may encounter:

| | |
|---|---|
| Alle richtingen | All directions |
| Andere richtingen | Other directions |
| Beschadigd wegdek | Bad road surface |
| Doorgand verkeer | Through traffic |
| Eenrichtingverkeer | One-way street |
| Langzaam rijden | Slow |
| Moeilijke doorgang | Obstruction ahead |
| Opgelet! | Caution! |
| Tol | Toll |
| Wegomlegging | Detour |
| Zachte berm | Soft shoulder |
| Are we on the right road for …? | Zijn wij op de juiste weg naar …? |
| Fill the tank, please | Vol, graag |
| Check the oil/tyres/ battery | Kijkt u even de olie/banden/ accu na |
| I've broken down | Ik heb autopech |

# E

## ELECTRICITY

Belgium operates on 230 volts, 50 Hz AC, requiring standard two-pin round continental plugs. Visitors should bring their own adapters.

## EMBASSIES AND CONSULATES (ambassades; consulaten)

All the foreign embassies and consulates are in Brussels.

**Australia:** rue Guimard 6–8, 1040 Brussels, tel: 02-286 05 00, www.belgium.embassy.gov.au.

**Canada:** avenue de Tervueren 2, 1040 Brussels, tel: 02-741 06 11, www.canadainternational.gc.ca/belgium-belgique/index.aspx.

**Ireland:** chaussée d'Etterbeek 180, 1040 Brussels, tel: 02-282 34 00, www.embassyofireland.be.

**New Zealand:** avenue des Nerviens 9–31, 1040 Brussels, tel: 02-512 10 40, www.nzembassy.com/belgium.

**South Africa:** rue Montoyer 17–19, 1000 Brussels, tel: 02-285 44 00, www.southafrica.be.

**UK:** avenue d'Auderghem 10, 1000 Brussels, tel: 02-287 62 11, http://ukinbelgium.fco.gov.uk/en.

**US:** boulevard du Régent 27, 1000 Brussels, tel: 02-508 21 11, www.usembassy.be.

## EMERGENCIES (noodgeval; see also HEALTH and POLICE)

The three-digit emergency telephone numbers listed below are valid throughout Belgium:

| | |
|---|---|
| **Emergency/police** | 101 |
| **Accidents** | 112 |
| **Fire brigade/ambulance** | 100 |

| | |
|---|---|
| I need a doctor/dentist/hospital | **Ik heb een arts/tandarts nodig/ziekenhuis** |

## GAY AND LESBIAN TRAVELLERS

For information on the gay, lesbian and bisexual scene in Bruges, contact Jong & Holebi in Brugge, Koningin Elisabethlaan 92, tel: 050-33 69 70, www.j-h.be. For the wider scene in Flanders, contact Holebifoon, tel: 0800-99 533, www.holebifoon.be.

## GETTING THERE

**By air.** Brussels Airport *(see page 112)* is linked by direct flights with major airlines from all European and many North American cities, but other long-distance travellers may have to connect via Amsterdam, London or Paris. Brussels Airlines (tel: 02-723 23 45, www.brusselsairlines.com), is the main local carrier. British Airways (tel: 0844-493 0787 in the UK, tel: 02-717 32 17 in Belgium, www.ba.com) flies from several UK airports to Brussels; flight time from London is about one hour. Several other airlines fly from UK airports to Brussels. They include BMI (tel: 0844-848 4888 in the UK, tel: 02-713 12 84 in Belgium, www.flybmi.com); and KLM (tel: 0871-231 0000 in the UK, tel: 070-22 53 35 in Belgium, www.klm.com). Aer Lingus (tel: 0818-365 000 in Ireland, tel: 070-35 99 01 in Belgium, www.aerlingus.com) has regular service to Brussels from Dublin. Ryanair (tel: 0871-246 000 in the UK, tel: 0818-30 30 30 in Ireland, tel: 0902-33 660 in Belgium, www.ryanair.com flies from airports in Britain and Ireland to Charleroi, near Brussels.

From the United States, American Airlines (tel: 800-433 7300 in the US, tel: 02-711 99 69 in Belgium, www.aa.com); Delta Air Lines (tel: 800-241 4141 in the US, tel: 02-711 97 99, www.delta.com); United Airlines (tel: 800-538 2929 in the US, tel: 02-713 36 00 in Belgium, www.united.com); and Continental Airlines (tel: 800-231 0856 in the US, tel: 0800-20 00 in Belgium, www.continental.com) all offer flights to Brussels. From Canada, Air Canada (tel: 888-247 2262 in Canada, tel: +31 20-405 52 50 in Holland, www.aircanada.ca) flies to Brussels.

**By rail.** Brussels and Bruges have excellent rail connections with the rest of the European network. There are various discounts for EU residents, and it is best to contact your local rail operator for the latest information before your trip.

From the UK it is possible to reach Bruges and Ghent easily using the Eurostar service through the Channel Tunnel. Trains depart from St Pancras International in London or Ashford International in Kent and arrive in Brussels within three hours. You can be in Bruges or Ghent in just over four hours. Check-in time at St Pancras is just 20 minutes before departure (and is strictly applied, so make sure you arrive on time), and your bags are with you at all times, so there is no delay waiting for luggage once you arrive. Trains are comfortable, and pay phones are located in every carriage. Passport controls are at your final destination only; don't forget your passport.

Seats should be reserved well in advance: this can be done direct (tel: 08432-186 186, www.eurostar.com) or at some mainline stations and travel agents. If you travel by Eurostar to Brussels and book your hotel through Belgian Tourist Reservations (tel: +32 2-513 74 84), you may be entitled to a discount on your accommodation in Bruges.

If you want to take your car, Eurotunnel trains travel via the Channel between Folkestone and Calais every 15 minutes. Passengers stay with their car for the 35-minute journey. Tel: 08443- 353 535, www.eurotunnel.com.

**By bus.** Eurolines (tel: 08705-143 219 in the UK, tel: 02-274 13 50 in Belgium, ww2w.eurolines.com) operates bus services between all major European cities and Brussels; those coming from London generally stop in Bruges.

**By boat.** There are car ferry crossings daily to Belgium from the UK (Hull to Zeebrugge) with P&O Ferries (tel: 0871-664 5645 in the UK, tel: 070-70 77 71 in Belgium, www.poferries.com); and three times a day (Ramsgate to Ostend) with Transeuropa Ferries (tel: 01843-595 522 in the UK, tel: +44 208-127 8303 from Belgium, www.transeuropaferries.com).

## GUIDES AND TOURS (gids; tolk; see BUDGETING FOR YOUR TRIP)

Guided tours allow you to explore parts of the city that you might not discover on your own. Groups and individuals can book qualified and very informative guides in advance from the tourist office, for a minimum two-hour tour. During July and August there are daily guided tours of the city, starting at 3pm from the tourist office (tel: 050-44 46 46).

Bruges's canals can be explored from 10am–6pm daily in the summer (only at weekends and holidays in winter). Boats depart from Rozenhoedkaai, Dijver and Mariastraat. Night tours for groups can also be arranged on request, and can be very appealing. It can be chilly on these tour boats, and even on a warm summer day you may be grateful for a sweater or jacket.

A 50-minute tour round Bruges by bus with taped commentary in the language of your choice makes a good introduction to the city. Tours are operated by Sightseeing Line, tel: 050-35 50 24, www.citytour.be with minibuses departing from the Markt at regular intervals. The same line operates tours to Damme for different lengths of time, depending on the season: they also depart from the Markt and can include a free drink and pancake in Damme, and a return canal trip on the Lamme Goedzak paddle-boat.

Quasimodo, tel: 050-37 04 70, run minibus tours of the countryside and Flanders Fields, including a beer-themed itinerary. Horse-drawn carriage rides through the city centre depart from the Markt (occasionally from the Burg), with a 10-minute break for the horse at Minnewater. Commentary is provided by the driver.

Quasimundo (as opposed to Quasimodo above) run cycling tours in and around Bruges. Tours, which last 2½ hours, include provision of a mountain bike, guide, transport by bus, insurance and rain gear; tel: 050-33 07 75, www.quasimundo.eu.

## H

## HEALTH AND MEDICAL CARE (See also EMERGENCIES)

Travellers from EU countries should receive free medical treatment in Belgium on presentation of the European Health Insurance Card (EHIC), available from post offices or online (www.ehic.org.uk), but it is wise to take out extra travel insurance, which should cover illness, accident and lost luggage. For non-EU citizens, travel insurance is essential.

A Belgian pharmacy *(apotheek)* is identified by a green cross and should have a list in the window of nearby late-night chemist shops. Such lists are also published in the local weekend press.

Call police or tourist information office for telephone numbers of doctors on weekend and night duty.

For a hospital in Bruges, go to the AZ Sint-Jan, Ruddershove 10, tel: 050-45 21 11, www.azbrugge.be.

Where is the duty pharmacy?    **Waar is de dienstdoende apotheek?**

## L

## LANGUAGE

About 60 percent of the population living in Flanders – which covers roughly the northern half of Belgium – speak Flemish (Dutch) and this is the language you will most often hear in Bruges and Ghent. French is the language in Wallonia, southern Belgium, and a small percentage of the people in the eastern districts of the country speak German as their first language. Brussels is officially bilingual, but has more French than Dutch speakers. A German-speaking minority of around 70,000 lives in the eastern districts of the country.

English is spoken by many and should be at least partially understood by virtually everybody. Written and spoken Dutch is sometimes extremely similar to English; at other times there are no clues as to meaning. Menus may be printed in English as well as Dutch and French; if they are not, most members of staff will be happy to explain what things mean.

Although local road signs are in Dutch, be aware that in this bilingual country many towns bear different names in French. Brugge (Dutch) is *Bruges* in French; Gent/*Gand*; Ieper/*Ypres*; Oudenaarde/*Audenarde*; Antwerpen/*Anvers*.

| | |
|---|---|
| good evening | Goedenavond |
| goodbye | Dag/tot ziens |
| today | vandaag |
| yesterday/tomorrow | gisteren/morgen |
| day/week | dag/week |
| month/year | maand/jaar |
| left/right | links/rechts |
| cheap/expensive | goedkoop/duur |
| hot/cold | warm/koud |

## Days and Months

| | | | |
|---|---|---|---|
| Sunday | **Zondag** | January | **Januari** |
| Monday | **Maandag** | February | **Februari** |
| Tuesday | **Dinsdag** | March | **Maart** |
| Wednesday | **Woensdag** | April | **April** |
| Thursday | **Donderdag** | May | **Mei** |
| Friday | **Vrijdag** | June | **Juni** |
| Saturday | **Zaterdag** | July | **Juli** |
| | | August | **Augustus** |
| | | September | **September** |
| | | October | **Oktober** |
| | | November | **November** |
| | | December | **December** |

## Numbers

| | | | |
|---|---|---|---|
| 0 | nul | 16 | zestien |
| 1 | een | 17 | zeventien |
| 2 | twee | 18 | achttien |
| 3 | drie | 19 | negentien |
| 4 | vier | 20 | twintig |
| 5 | vijf | 21 | een en twintig |
| 6 | zes | 30 | dertig |
| 7 | zeven | 40 | veertig |
| 8 | acht | 50 | vijftig |
| 9 | negen | 60 | zestig |
| 10 | tien | 70 | zeventig |
| 11 | elf | 80 | tachtig |
| 12 | twaalf | 90 | negentig |
| 13 | dertien | 100 | honderd |
| 14 | veertien | 200 | tweehonderd |
| 15 | vijftien | 1,000 | duizend |

# M

## MAPS

Bruges tourist office produces a free comprehensive map of central Bruges, and several commercial maps can be bought at bookshops and newsagents around town.

## MEDIA

**Newspapers and magazines** *(kranten; tijdschriften)*
English-language publications are sold at station kiosks, larger bookshops and news-stands. Larger hotels may stock the *International Herald Tribune*, *Financial Times* and other international newspapers.

Have you any English newspapers? **Heeft u Engelse kranten?**

### Radio and television

BBC long-wave and world services and European-based American networks can be picked up easily. Most hotels have cable television with up to 30 channels, including BBC World News from the UK and CNN International from the US. Many European channels show English language films and programmes with subtitles.

## MONEY

### Currency

The unit of currency in Belgium is the euro, which is abbreviated to € and divided into 100 cents. Coins are: €2, €1, and 50, 20, 10, 5, 2 and 1 cents. Banknotes are in denominations of €500, 200, 100, 50, 20 10 and 5. The €500 and €200 notes are rarely if ever seen in circulation, and some small businesses may even be reluctant to accept €100 notes.

### Exchange facilities

There is a standard commission for changing foreign currency and traveller's cheques. Generally, banks offer the best rates, followed by bureaux de change. Hotels will often exchange currency, but at an inferior rate. Currency-exchange machines at Brussels Airport make transactions in several currencies. ATMs accepting non-Belgian debit and credit cards are widely available. The two Belgian ATM brand names – Bancontact and Mister Cash – are being phased out in favour of the Maestro brand, but this makes no difference in practice.

### Credit cards *(credit card)*

Major hotels and many restaurants and shops accept payment by international credit cards.

### Traveller's cheques *(reischeque)*

These are widely accepted and can be cashed as long as you have your passport with you.

**Sales tax, service charge**

Called BTW, a sales (value-added) tax is imposed on most goods and services in Belgium. In hotels and most restaurants, this is accompanied by a service charge. Both charges are included in the bill. To recover some of the tax on expensive purchases, look for shops displaying signs saying 'Europe Tax-Free Shopping' or 'Tax-Free International'; retailers are well acquainted with the necessary procedures.

| | |
|---|---|
| I want to change some pounds/dollars. | **Ik wil graag ponden/dollars wisselen.** |
| Do you accept travellers' cheques? | **Accepteert u reischeques?** |
| Can I pay with this credit card? | **Kan ik met deze credit card betalen?** |

O

**OPENING HOURS** (see also Public Holidays)

Banks open Monday–Friday 9am–noon, 2–4pm and some until 5pm. Some banks open on Saturday morning and until 6pm on one or two days a week.

Shops and department stores are generally open Monday–Saturday 9am–5.30pm or 10am–6pm. Many smaller shops close for an hour for lunch. Late-night shopping is on Friday until 7pm. Many stores are closed on Sunday.

Post offices are open Monday–Friday 9am–5pm. Larger post offices are also open on Saturday 9am–noon, smaller ones close for an hour at lunch time.

Museums are generally open Tuesday to Sunday from 9.30 or 10am to 5pm, but the smaller ones often close for an hour at lunch time. In Bruges, some may be closed on Tuesday or Wednesday during the low season.

# P

## POLICE (see also EMERGENCIES)

The *politie* or police can be reached on the emergency 101 phone number. They are not that much in evidence on the streets (there is seldom any need for them in Bruges), but they are usually dressed in dark blue. Any theft should be reported at the nearest police station. The main police station in Bruges is at Hauwerstraat 7, tel: 050-44 88 44.

| | |
|---|---|
| Where's the nearest police station? | **War is het dichtsbijzijnd politiebureau?** |

## POST OFFICES (posterijen)

The main post office in Bruges is at Markt 5. There are post offices in Ghent at Lange Kruisstraat 55 and Sint-Pietersstation. Opening times are Monday–Friday 9am–5pm and Saturday 9am–noon. Smaller post offices close for lunch from noon until 2pm.

Mail boxes are red, often decorated with a white bugle. They may be either free-standing or attached to walls. Stamps can also be purchased from souvenir shops selling postcards.

| | |
|---|---|
| A stamp for this letter/ postcard, please. | **Een postzegel voor deze brief/briefkaart, alstublieft.** |
| airmail | **luchtpost** |
| registered | **aangetekend** |

## PUBLIC HOLIDAYS (openbare feestdagen)

Most shops and other businesses are closed on public holidays; if museums are not closed, they will be operating on Sunday hours. If a holiday falls on a Sunday, the following Monday will usually be taken off instead.

| | | |
|---|---|---|
| 1 January | *Nieuwjaar* | New Year's Day |
| 1 May | *Dag van de Arbeid* | Labour Day |
| 21 July | *Nationalefeestdag* | National Day |
| 15 August | *Maria Hemelvaart* | Assumption |
| 1 November | *Allerheiligen* | All Saints' Day |
| 11 November | *Wapenstilstand* | Armistice Day |
| 25 December | *Kerstdag* | Christmas Day |
| Moveable dates: | *Paasmaandag* | Easter Monday |
| | *Hemelvaartsdag* | Ascension Day |
| | *Pinkstermaandag* | Whit Monday |

## R

## RELIGION

The population of Belgium is predominantly Roman Catholic, but Protestant churches are also well represented in both cities. In Bruges, there is an English church at Keersstraat 1 and an Ecumenical chapel at Ezelstraat 83.

## T

## TELEPHONES

The phone system in Belgium is reliable and extensive. Hotel phones are the most convenient, although they are also the most expensive. Public phone booths are plentiful, particularly in the city centres and railway stations; most of them can be used to phone direct overseas, and have instructions in English, French and German as well as Dutch. Many booths only accept phonecards rather than coins: cards can be purchased from post offices, news-stands and railway stations.

The dialling code for Belgium is 32; Brussels is 02, Bruges is 050, and Ghent is 09; you always need to use the local area code, even if you are calling from inside the area. The Yellow Pages directory *(Gouden Gids)* has a useful English-language index.

## TIME ZONES

The following chart shows the time difference between Belgium and various cities in winter. Between the beginning of April and the end of October Belgian clocks are put forward one hour.

| New York | London | **Belgium** | Jo'burg | Sydney | Auckland |
|----------|--------|-------------|---------|--------|----------|
| 6am | 11am | **noon** | 1pm | 10pm | midnight |

## TIPPING

In a country where service is included in most bills, tipping is not a problem. Most people will not expect a tip (but will appreciate it if you give them one). Exceptions include public toilets, where the attendant may expect a tip of 25–50 cents, and porter and maid service in the more expensive hotels.

## TOILETS

A toilet is generally called a WC (pronounced vay-say) in Flanders. If there is not a graphic of some kind that leaves no room for doubt about which toilet is for females and which for males, look for the words *dames* (women) and *heren* (men). In small cafés and restaurants, men's and women's toilets may be only notionally separated.

## TOURIST INFORMATION

**United Kingdom:** Tourism Flanders-Brussels, 1a Cavendish Square, London W1G 0LD, tel: 020-7307 7738, www.visitflanders.co.uk.
**US:** Belgian Tourist Office, 220 East 42nd Street, Suite 3402, New York, NY 10017, tel: 212-758 8130, www.visitbelgium.com.
**Canada:** English-speaking residents can contact the New York office *(see above)*, and by calling tel: 514-457 2888.

The information office in Bruges is in the Concertgebouw, 't Zand 34, tel: 050-44 46 46, email: toerisme@brugge.be, www.brugge. be, open daily 10am–1pm, 1.30–6pm during the summer, 9.30am– 5pm in winter. There is also a tourist information office at the railway station, where you can book hotel accommodation in the city (closed Sunday and Monday).

The free monthly newsletter, *Exit*, and brochure, *events@brugge*, are available in English from the tourist offices, which also offer a free monthly newspaper, *Brugge Cultuurmagazine*. It is in Dutch, but performance dates and venue details are fairly easy to understand.

In Ghent, the tourist office is in the crypt of the Belfort in Botermarkt, tel: 09-266 56 60, email: visit@gent.be, www.visitgent.be. It is open during the summer months Monday–Friday 9.30am–6.30pm, Saturday–Sunday and public holidays 10am–noon and 2pm–6.30pm. In the winter, hours are Monday–Friday 9.30am–4.30pm, Saturday–Sunday 9.30am–1pm.

Where is the tourist office?  **Waar is het toeristen-bureau?**

## TRANSPORT (see also BUDGETING FOR YOUR TRIP)

In cities where everything seems to be a short walk away, public transport is not usually a problem.

### Buses

In Bruges, buses to the suburbs can be caught most conveniently in the Markt or at the railway station. Sightseeing buses and excursions also depart from the Markt. Other main bus stops are at Wollestraat, Biekorf and Kuipersstraat. A one-day pass (€5 if bought before boarding, €6 on board the bus) allows unlimited travel on all the city's buses. Regional buses (to destinations outside Bruges) can be caught at the railway station and in 't Zand. A helpline is available for both types of bus on 070-22 02 00, and schedules are also displayed in the tourist information office *(see page 131)*.

In Ghent, the main bus station is outside Sint-Pieters railway station. This is also a terminus for many of the city's trams, which serve most of Ghent and are great fun to ride. Buses and trams can also be caught from the city centre, at Korenmarkt.

| When is the next bus/ train to…? | Wanneer vertrekt de volgende bus/trein naar…? |
| I want a ticket to… | Ik wil graag een kaart naar… |
| one way (single) | enkele reis |
| round-trip (return) | retour |
| first/second class | eerste/tweede klas |

**Taxis**

Taxis are plentiful in both Bruges and Ghent, where they flock together outside the railway stations for the hotel run. Order your taxi at the hotel when you check out, and one will arrive in two or three minutes. However, taxis are rather more difficult to hail in the streets – in Bruges, you are most likely to find one in the Markt, while in Ghent, the best place to try hailing a taxi is Korenmarkt.

**Trains**

The Belgian railway network is superb. Bruges and Ghent are situated on the same line that connects Brussels with Ostend. Train services are prompt and frequent. Announcements on inter-city trains are given in Dutch, French and English, and text-screen panels in each carriage give the name of the next station. Information and assistance are available at both cities' railway stations.

There are first- and second-class carriages and smoking and non-smoking sections (although smoking carriages are likely to be phased out soon). A range of discounts are offered at weekends and on long-term passes.

▼

## VISAS AND ENTRY REQUIREMENTS

Visitors from EU countries only need an identity card (or passport) to enter Belgium. Citizens of most other countries including the US, Canada, Australia and New Zealand must have a valid passport.

European and North American residents are not subject to any health requirements. In case of doubt, check with Belgian representatives in your own country before departure.

As Belgium is a member of the European Union (EU), free exchange of non-duty-free goods for personal use is permitted between Belgium and the UK and Ireland.

**Currency restrictions.** There is no limit on the amount of euros or other currency that can be brought into or taken out of the country by non-residents.

# W

## WEBSITES

Useful general information can be found at www.visitbelgium.com and www.visitflanders.co.uk, and the tourist boards for both Bruges and Ghent operate easy to navigate websites giving information on hotels, attractions, and more, www.brugge.be and www.visitgent.be. Useful sites for planning your travel arrangements are www.b-rail.be and www.brusselsairport.be. In addition, most hotels have their own websites *(see Recommended Hotels, page 135)*.

# Y

## YOUTH HOSTELS

Bruges and its immediate neighbourhood have a number of 'Youth Hotels' and Youth Hostels. There are three located in the city itself, notably:

Bauhaus International Youth Hotel, Langestraat 135–7, 8000 Bruges, tel: 050-34 10 93, www.bauhaus.be.

The Passage, Dweersstraat 26, 8000 Bruges, tel: 050-34 02 32, www.passagebruges.com.

Snuffel Sleep-in, Ezelstraat 47–9, 8000 Bruges, tel: 050-33 31 33, www.snuffel.be.

# Recommended Hotels

With more than 100 hotels throughout the city, Bruges has a wide range of establishments and locations. Hotels that are part of an international chain will provide a predictable degree of comfort, but guests may miss out on the more authentic Flemish hospitality offered by locally run establishments. The tourist information office provides brochures listing hotels. It is always advisable to book in advance. Bruges is particularly crowded in the summer, tending to be busiest at weekends. If you trust to luck and arrive with no place to stay, go straight to the tourist office *(see page 131)*, which can almost guarantee to find you something.

Prices are based on the cost per night of a double room with en suite bath or shower, including service charge, sales tax and breakfast. Rates can vary according to the season or time of the week. All the hotels listed here accept major credit cards.

| | |
|---|---|
| € | below 100 euros |
| €€ | 100–200 euros |
| €€€ | 200–300 euros |
| €€€€ | above 300 euros |

## BRUGES

**Acacia €€** *Korte Zilverstraat 3A–5, 8000 Bruges, tel: 050-34 44 11, www.hotel-acacia.com.* This comfortable modern hotel (part of the Best Western chain) is centrally located just off the Markt. All rooms have a private bathroom, television, kitchenette, minibar, radio, telephone and safe. Health club, swimming pool, solarium.

**Azalea €€** *Wulfhagestraat 43, 8000 Bruges, tel: 050-33 14 78, www.azaleahotel.be.* Family-run hotel in a 14th-century house on the banks of the Speelmansrei canal, 200m/yds from the Markt. Comfortably furnished, with a lovely Art Nouveau staircase.

**Bauhaus Budget Hotel €** *Langestraat 135–7, tel: 050-34 10 93, www.bauhaus.be.* This decent low-cost hotel, close to the eastern ring canal park, might not win many design awards, but rooms ranging in size from singles to quads, and an atmospheric bar-restaurant, are undoubted draws for the youthful clientele that shows up here.

**Best Western Premier Hotel Navarra Brugge €€€** *Sint-Jakobsstraat 41, 8000 Bruges, tel: 050-34 05 61, www.hotelnavarra.com.* Housed in a mansion that used to be a royal residence in the 17th century – albeit 'only' of a prince – this thoroughly modernised hotel treats its guests like minor royalty. You can relax in the garden and kick back in the wellness centre.

**Bourgoensche Cruyce €€€** *Wollestraat 41–3, 8000 Bruges, tel: 050-33 79 26, www.bourgoenschecruyce.be.* This is a tiny, charming wooden-fronted hotel (just 16 rooms) in a superb canalside location. Rooms are decorated in sumptuous 17th-century Flemish style with carved antique furniture, stone floors and large fireplaces. It featured in the 2008 hit film *In Bruges*.

**Bryghia €€** *Oosterlingenplein 4; tel: 050-33 80 59; www.bryghia hotel.be.* This friendly, family-run hotel is situated in a peaceful neighbourhood, rarely visited by tourists. Part of it occupies a 15th-century building that once belonged to Hanseatic merchants. The interior is cosy and tastefully furnished with comfortable sofas and wood beams. Some rooms enjoy a view of a sleepy canal.

**Cavalier €** *Kuipersstraat 25, 8000 Bruges, tel: 050-33 02 07, www.hotelcavalier.be.* In spite of its slightly ramshackle external appearance, this small hotel (eight rooms) behind the city theatre is friendly and ordered and offers good value in the cheaper range of hotels.

**Central €€** *Markt 30, 8000 Bruges, tel: 050-33 18 05, www. hotelcentral.be.* The name is entirely appropriate, since it would be hard to imagine a more central location in Bruges than on the Markt, directly facing the Belfry. This small hotel has rooms quite a bit more elegant than the rustic setting would suggest, and there is a fine restaurant with a terrace on the square.

**Crowne Plaza Bruges €€€** *Burg 10, 8000 Bruges, tel: 050-44 68 44, www.ichotelsgroup.com.* Centrally located, peaceful de luxe hotel. Well-equipped bedrooms, many with views of the historic Burg. In an intriguing blend of ancient and modern, the building incorporates the foundations of the demolished medieval St Donatian's Cathedral, part of the 10th-century city wall and a 16th-century cellar.

**De Tuilerieen €€€** *Dijver 7, 8000 Bruges, tel: 050-34 36 91, www.hoteltuilerieen.com.* The hotel is ideally situated just a few doors away from the main museums and with fine views of the Dijver canal from the front rooms. Pool, sauna, and solarium.

**Die Swaene €€€** *Steenhouwersdijk 1, 8000 Bruges, tel: 050-34 27 98, www.dieswaene.com.* This is a lovely romantic hotel with charming, attentive staff and rooms elegantly and individually furnished to a high standard. The lounge was originally the Guild Hall of the Tailors. Some of the rooms are in a separate wing, called the Canal House.

**Duc de Bourgogne €€** *Huidenvettersplein 12, 8000 Bruges, tel: 050-33 20 38, www.ducdebourgogne.be.* This small hotel occupies an attractive step-gabled house in historic Huidenvettersplein (Tanners' Square), right in the heart of the city. The hotel is elegantly, if a little over-ornately, decorated, with lots of tapestries adorning the walls and lavish antique furniture.

**Egmond €€** *Minnewater 15, 8000 Bruges, tel: 050-34 14 45, www.egmond.be.* There are just eight rooms in this hotel, which occupies a large 18th-century mansion with its own gardens, beside the Minnewater Park, giving it a tranquil, rural ambience. The rooms are furnished in traditional style and look out over the park.

**Erasmus €€** *Wollestraat 35, 8000 Bruges, tel: 050-33 57 81, www.hotelerasmus.com.* A small establishment with a breezily informal atmosphere and rooms that are nicely though not luxuriously furnished, the Erasmus is well-situated in the centre of town. There is a fine traditional Belgian restaurant and a bar that sells a range of artisanal Belgian beers.

**Fevery €** *Collaert Mansionstraat 3, 8000 Bruges, tel: 050-33 12 69, www.hotelfevery.be.* A small, friendly family-run hotel in an extremely quiet location just off Langerei, the long canal that reaches towards the north of the city. Bikes are available for hire.

**Graaf van Vlaanderen €** *'t Zand 19, 8000 Bruges, tel: 050-33 31 50, www.graafvanvlaanderen.be.* A good budget choice, this small, family-run hotel has pleasant rooms, a bustling restaurant and tea-room, and a lively atmosphere emanating from the nightlife possibilities on its doorstep.

**Heritage €€** *Niklaas Desparsstraat 11, 8000 Bruges, tel: 050-44 44 44, www.heritage-com.be.* A hotel that delivers country-manor style in an old Bruges town house that has a decorated ceiling with a chandelier in the breakfast room. The rooms are relatively small but luxuriously appointed. There's an excellent restaurant serving French-Flemish food.

**Jan Brito €€** *Freren Fonteinstraat 1, 8000 Bruges, tel: 050-33 06 01, www.janbrito.eu.* Beautifully restored 16th-century mansion, full of period detail, situated just a short walk away from the city's major attractions.

**Lucca €** *Naaldenstraat 30, 8000 Bruges, tel: 050-34 20 67, www.hotellucca.be.* Housed in a building that stands atop a 14th-century cellar once used by Italian traders from Lucca, this fine little hotel offers a lot of traditional atmosphere in its breakfast room and other public spaces, and plain character in the rooms.

**Martin's Orangerie €€€€** *Kartuizerinnenstraat 10, 8000 Bruges, tel: 050-34 16 49, www.martins-hotels.com.* This luxurious hotel is wonderfully situated on the banks of the canal opposite Dijver. The rooms are all individually furnished, with lavish marble bathrooms. Breakfast on the canalside verandah on a warm summer morning is a real delight.

**Martin's Relais Oud Huis Amsterdam €€€€** *Spiegelrei 3, 8000 Bruges, tel: 050-34 18 10, www.martins-hotels.com.* A rambling canalside building, parts of which date from the 14th century, are the setting for this fine hotel with large, ornate rooms. Those in the front have a canal view and those at the back look out onto a court-yard and garden. There is a wooden staircase, chandeliers and oak beams and a pretty interior courtyard.

**Montanus €€** *Nieuwe Gentweg 76–8, 8000 Bruges, tel: 050-33 11 76, www.montanus.be.* Tasteful, restrained elegance in a historic house. In addition to the bedrooms, there are colonial-style pavil-ion rooms inside the house, and a cedarwood honeymoon suite in the serene private garden.

**NH Brugge €€€** *Boeveriestraat 2, 8000 Bruges, tel: 050-44 97 11, www.nh-hotels.com.* Large rooms and an atmospheric setting in a 300-year-old monastery just off the bustling 't Zand Square add character to this large and well-equipped hotel, which has its own heated indoor swimming pool.

**The Pand Hotel €€€** *Pandreitje 16, 8000 Bruges, tel: 050-34 06 66, www.pandhotel.com.* Old-fashioned furnishings complement modern conveniences and lend an authentic touch to the rooms in this quiet hotel set in an 18th-century mansion near the Markt. The excellent breakfasts are cooked on a cast-iron range in the break-fast room.

**Prinsenhof €€€** *Ontvangersstraat 9, 8000 Bruges, tel: 050-34 26 90, www.prinsenhof.be.* This elegant hotel is traditionally furnished, with wood panelling, chandeliers, and antiques; it also has excel-lent bathrooms. There's a warm atmosphere, and possibly the best breakfast in Bruges.

**Rosenburg €€** *Coupure 30, 8000 Bruges, tel: 050-34 01 94, www.rosenburg.be.* A quiet hotel situated on the banks of a canal approximately a 10-minute walk from the centre of Bruges. The atmosphere in this modern brick building is relaxed and friendly – staff are particularly helpful.

**Ter Brughe €€** *Oost-Gistelhof 2, 8000 Bruges, tel: 050-34 03 24, www.hotelterbrughe.com.* Extremely attractive hotel in the elegant St Giles quarter, five minutes' walk from the centre of Bruges. Breakfast is served in the 14th-century beamed and vaulted cellar, which was once a warehouse for goods brought along the canal.

**Ter Duinen €€** *Langerei 52, 8000 Bruges, tel: 050-33 04 37, www.terduinenhotel.be.* This pleasant waterfront hotel set along the canal stretching northeast from the city centre offers a good compromise between essential facilities and cost, modern fittings and traditional looks.

**Walburg €€€** *Boomgaardstraat 13–15, 8000 Bruges, tel: 050-34 94 14, www.hotelwalburg.be.* Spacious, elegant hotel in a fine, recently restored historic mansion just 100m/yds from the Burg. All 13 rooms – which are larger than average for the city – have large, Italian marble bathrooms, and high ceilings and elaborate cornices abound.

## GHENT

**Best Western Residence Hotel Cour Saint Georges €€** *Botermarkt 2, 9000 Ghent, tel: 09-224 24 24, www.courstgeorges.com.* Most of the rooms at this hotel are actually in a modern, rather basic annexe situated across the road from the ancient building (originally the house used by the Guild of Crossbowmen), which dates back to 1228.

**The Boatel €€** *Voorhoutkaai 44, 9000 Ghent, tel: 09-267 10 30, www.theboatel.com.* A unique place to stay in Ghent, in one of the few cabins on board this floating hotel boat, moored on the river Leie, just 600m/yds from the main railway station. Seven rooms.

**Flandria Centrum €** *Barrestraat 3–7, 9000 Ghent, tel: 09-223 06 26, www.flandria-centrum.be.* Cheap, basic hotel in a quiet side street close to the cathedral. Ideal for those on a shoestring budget looking only for a place to sleep, wash and change their clothes. Substantial breakfasts and friendly staff. Some disabled access. 16 rooms.

**Ghent River Hotel €€€€** *Waaistraat 5, tel: 09-266 10 10, www. ghent-river-hotel.be.* This stylish waterfront hotel near the Vrijdagmarkt evokes the trading history of Ghent. Some rooms occupy a restored 19th-century sugar factory, while others are in a 16th-century town house; the square was the site of a yarn market in the Middle Ages and the 19th century. When booking, ask for one of the rooms in the former factory, as these have oak beams, brick walls and odd industrial implements used for decoration. The rooms in the modern extension are plainer. The hotel has a rooftop breakfast room with striking views of the old city, a jetty and a fitness room.

**Gravensteen €€** *Jan Breydelstraat 35, 9000 Ghent, tel: 09-225 11 50, www.gravensteen.be.* This 19th-century mansion, once the home of an industrial magnate, has been turned into one of the city's most elegant yet friendly hotels. It is situated across the water from the Gravensteen castle, of which the rooms at the front have a fine view, and it has been tastefully renovated and extended. There is a fitness room and sauna.

**Monasterium €€€** *Oude Houtlei 56, 9000 Ghent, tel: 09-269 22 10, www.monasterium.be.* This original hotel recently opened in a converted 19th-century neo-Gothic convent. As well as standard modern rooms, it offers some simple cheaper rooms (**€–€€**) in the adjoining Guesthouse PoortAckere. Located in what were formerly nuns' cells, these rooms are fairly basic but ideal for budget travellers. Breakfast (extra charge) is served in an ornate refectory.

**NH Gent-Belfort €€€** *Hoogpoort 63, 9000 Ghent, tel: 09-233 33 31, www.nh-hotels.com.* Superbly located opposite the Stadhuis, the Gent-Belfort offers excellent value for a hotel of this quality. The rooms are well appointed and extremely comfortable, with splendid bathrooms. One of the two bars is in an historic crypt. There is a fitness room and sauna.

# INDEX

**Berlitz** pocket guide

# Bruges & Ghent

**Sixth Edition 2011**

Written by Jack Messenger and Brigitte Lee
Updated by George McDonald
Series Editor: Tom Stainer

Photography credits
All Pictures APA Glyn Genin except:

APA Pete Bennett 42, 81, 84
APA Chris Coe 8, 16, 19, 26, 59, 64, 69, 73, 76,
82, 97
APA Jerry Dennis 3TL, 7M, 34, 50, 87
Flanders Tourism 88
Tony Halliday 7B, 18, 22, 49, 53, 55, 56, 70,
Istockphoto 66
Scala 13, 15,
Bert Snijders 92
Superstock 80

Cover picture: 4Corners Images

Every effort has been made to provide
accurate information in this publication,
but changes are inevitable. The
publisher cannot be responsible for any resulting
loss, inconvenience or injury.

**Contact us**

At Berlitz we strive to keep our guides as
accurate and up to date as possible, but if you
find anything that has changed, or if you have
any suggestions on ways to improve this guide,
then we would be delighted to hear from you.

Berlitz Publishing, PO Box 7910,
London SE1 1WE, England.
email: berlitz@apaguide.co.uk
www.berlitzpublishing.com